THE DYNAMOS

THE DYNAMOS

WHO ARE THEY ANYWAY?

BRETT KINGSTONE

JOHN WILEY & SONS
New York / Chichester / Brisbane / Toronto / Singapore

Library of Congress Cataloging in Publication Data:

Kingstone, Brett.
The dynamos: who are they anyway?

   Bibliography: p.
   Includes index.
   1. Businessmen—United States—Biography.
   2. Entrepreneur—United States   3. New business
   enterprises—United States—Management.   I. Title
HC102.5.A2K56 1987   338'.04'0922 [B]   87-1754
ISBN 0-471-85827-7

TO JOHN F. CADE

CADE INDUSTRIES, EDAC TECHNOLOGIES

1949–1986

WHOSE LIFE SYMBOLIZED THE SPIRIT OF THIS BOOK.
HE DREAMED GREAT DREAMS AND HAD THE COURAGE
TO LIVE THEM.

On January 27, 1986, the day before the space shuttle disaster, a twin-engine Cessna belonging to John Cade, our close friend and business associate, went down over Troy, Michigan, en route to John's factory near Lansing. John and his pilot were both killed. To us another hero had been lost, another person who showed us how to reach for the stars.

Cade was the founder and chairman of Cade Industries, an aerospace company that had grown, under his leadership, from sales of a few hundred thousand dollars to over $10 million in a few years. Our investment firm, Kingstone Prato, Inc., had worked alongside the New York firm of James J. Duane to orchestrate Cade's public acquisition financing, through which he acquired Gros-Ite Corporation, with annual sales exceeding $40 million. Cade pulled off an amazing feat. Starting from nothing, within three years he had built an aerospace conglomerate that included two publicly held companies, Cade Industries and EDAC Technologies (formerly Gros-Ite), totaling over $50 million in sales. Only a few months after accomplishing the greatest achievement of his career, Cade's life was ended by the tragic accident.

We all would have expected John Cade to die in the saddle, but in his office at the age of 99, not in a plane crash when he was only 37. John Cade personified our dreams and proved that we can live them. He had much more ahead of him in life, and the realization that we can no longer share the joy of his accomplishments is especially saddening.

Cade was a true dynamo. His life was exemplary and represents the spirit of this book. His story is here among the dynamos as our tribute to him and in written memory for his loving family: his wife Molly and his children Christian, Julie, Brian, and Kevin. We dedicate this book to our friend in the knowledge that John's dreams will live on. They will remain as an inspiration for all our endeavors.

A MESSAGE FROM
ARTHUR LIPPER III

Flattery will get you everything. That's a lesson Brett Kingstone
has learned well. Brett, the stereotypical entrepreneur's entrepreneur, the superactive, high energy level, always confident, telephone-dependent, able communicator and self-
promoter (in the best sense of the term) appealed to my well-
known and enlarged ego by requesting me to write something
that would appear in connection with his latest book. I agreed,
as not to yield to Brett's charm and energy would have deprived
me of an opportunity to latch onto his star.

The Dynamos is a book about winners. Brett is about winners,
and the readers will have to be interested in winning to find
the book interesting. The book is not so much a how-to, but
rather a how-I-did-it report of the history and techniques
used by those selected to be profiled.

There is as much to be learned by a careful reading of the
stories as there is in many graduate business courses. The
knowledgeable reader can see the mistakes coming and the
less experienced reader will understand them once the story
develops. After all, understanding mistakes is what profit
education (the mission of *Venture* magazine) is all about.

I first met Brett through the Association of College Entrepreneurs, or ACE, its appropriate acronym. ACE is the most

amazing collection of high-energy, focused, motivated, dream-driven entrepreneurs ever assembled. There is pure magic in being in contact with these young people, and Brett both chronicles and represents the best of them.

I love promoters, being one myself. Promoters are those people who have a product to sell, one that may be only themselves, and who do so with confidence and enthusiasm. *The Dynamos* is about promoters and entrepreneurs. Not all entrepreneurs are promoters, but most successful entrepreneurs have promotional instincts and do a pretty good job of selling themselves to themselves and others.

There is one word that comes to mind in connection with the book and Brett. That word is irrepressible.

If you want your kids to understand motivation and perhaps become motivated themselves, let them read *The Dynamos*. If you want to understand the phenomenon of our times, the young entrepreneur, read the book. If you are frightened by change and crave the status quo, you will not like *The Dynamos*.

The Dynamos is a natural candidate for a television series. The subjects of *The Dynamos* are visual and vital people. Theirs is a visual story. I think *Venture* will do the series unless someone else gets there first.

ARTHUR LIPPER III, CHAIRMAN
Venture Magazine

PREFACE

We begin our introduction with a little story about two entrepreneurs, Bob and Sam. Bob and Sam started out on two completely different paths only to find themselves later having their paths meet or should we say "merge." After receiving his degree at a famous western university, Bob went off to participate in a number of new ventures, while Sam was out somewhere farther east learning how investors view entrepreneurs from the other side of the fence.

After receiving his MBA in corporate finance and learning the tools of high finance from the lofty headquarters of Prudential's corporate finance department in Newark, New Jersey, Sam decided to head West. Why West? Well, Sam was tiring of the big corporate world and wanted to go where the "action" is. While at Prudential he worked on a number of financings of oil projects in Billings, Montana, so he decided that, for now at least, Billings, Montana is where the "action" is. With that Sam loaded up his 280Z with all his worldly possessions, mainly his books and files, and headed for Billings.

Soon after arriving in Billings, Sam was to learn that although there were a few oil rigs in town, there was indeed nothing else. After convincing himself that Billings was not where the "action" is, he decided to head for the nearest major city, Denver.

After arriving in Denver and reviewing the local want ads in the *Denver Post*, Sam soon found himself working for a rather notorious little oil tycoon whose idea of a hostile takeover included the use of armed guards and various forms of breaking and entry. After viewing the rather interesting behavior of his new employer, Sam decided that, for now, this is where the "action" is. He proceeded to justify his rather immense new salary reduction (he started at $800 a week, much less than MBA salary grade at "The Pru") by first uttering his almost famous and rather often repeated statement that "in life sometimes you have to take a step back in order to make a great leap forward." Sam was later to learn that his employer founded Greece's offshore oil production through funding provided by a Denver "Penny Stock" offering, which suffered through a few rounds of nationalizations and ultimately rebounded from Chapter 11 to build one of the most successful independently owned oil wildcatters in the country.

Meanwhile somewhere in the San Francisco Bay area, Bob was busy getting his head handed to him by a famous big Wall Street tycoon in his first investment banking endeavor. The tycoon was soon to teach Bob that a deal is never done until the check clears the bank and that all handshakes and agreements on Wall Street are subject to market conditions. Bob later grew very fond of the tycoon and realized that he was teaching him some of the most important lessons that he would learn.

While Bob was discovering the realities of racing down Wall Street, Sam had long since learned how even the toughest of those games are played and had moved his corporate finance advisory service to the offices of a well-known Denver stock buyer and venture capitalist. It seems that most of the sharks in the waters seem to know each other, regardless of in what ocean they swim, and as fate would have it Sam was soon sent to an undisclosed location in the San Francisco Bay area to check out a little "high tech" company that had just filed to go public. It is there he happened to meet Bob. During that meeting Sam tried to inform Bob of life's realities in another one of his almost famous and often repeated statements, "In this business you're either one of two things: a shark or shark bait."

Two plane flights later, Sam convinced Bob that Colorado is destined to become the new financial capital of the world (the only problem is Colorado doesn't realize it yet), and the two abandoned their current endeavors to join forces to venture off into the great unknown. The public offering never happened—Bob put a private placement together instead and Sam upon trying to enlist the support of his employer in his new venture was rewarded with a pink slip on his desk the next day. So they set off together on their own, knowing that although they may have lost the initial battle, ultimately they would win the war. Patience, dedication, enthusiasm, and youth were the greatest weapons in their arsenal—particularly youth. Specifically because one of the ways you can almost be assured of winning the war is by simply outliving your older and wiser opponents.

Bob and Sam set out to learn about other young adventurers along the way. They met many young people who at an early age built exciting new companies which they hoped to help finance. Bob and Sam would often refer to these young men and women as "dynamos" and believed that these people were the ones who "make things happen" and ultimately will be the people who will guide our economy during the next few decades.

To our friends, it should be at least more than a hint by now that Bob and Sam are actually Brett Kingstone and Steven Prato. Steve was my partner in the founding of an investment firm and he was very influential in the creation of this book.

Perhaps Steve Prato best indicated what we were looking for in a "dynamo" in our selections for this book when in a speech to a venture capital group he described what we were looking for as an investment firm: "It is this entrepreneurial niche that Kingstone Prato evolved to play within. It is a world of interaction with achievers with limitless dreams. It is a world where separating the winners from the losers is the key to making a fortune. . . . We set up an investment bank to cater to young, dynamic businesspeople who had a clear vision of where they were going but needed capital to get there." As Jeff Moritz, one of the dynamos described in the book, says, "With the right idea, the right people, and sufficient capital, you can accomplish almost *anything*."

In the 1968 bestseller by Ferdinand Lundberg, *The Rich and the Super-Rich*, the author says, "The day of accumulating gargantuan new personal fortunes in the United States is just about ended." He had no idea how wrong he would turn out to be. The 1980s have created more opportunities for amassing large fortunes at an early age than was ever possible previously. This book is testimony to that fact. Steven and I traveled all over the country meeting dynamic young businesspeople in every industry. We found that the people behind the success stories were even younger than their counterparts of a few years before, and that more people were acquiring an impressive amount of business savvy at an early age. Unlike their older predecessors, our dynamos never complained about the economy or foreign competition—they just wanted to be free of red tape and bureaucratic restrictions so they could charge full speed ahead. Our dynamos are people who are willing to live their dreams, take risks, make mistakes, and pick themselves up to press on with a burning desire to achieve.

BRETT KINGSTONE

Boulder, Colorado
March 1987

ACKNOWLEDGMENTS

The fact that I am still alive and in one piece is mostly due to the good graces and immense patience of my secretary and office manager Ginger Howell. Rumor has it that during the numerous rewrites and insane deadlines forced upon her by this book, she was overheard at her bible study class asking the Lord to free her from thoughts regarding the disposal of my body. Ms. Howell has been a great help on both the preparation and development of the manuscript. I owe her a great debt of gratitude both for her hard work and sincere friendship. Also thanks to Judson Main for his contribution to the typing of the manuscript. I am convinced that Judson is the world's fastest word processor.

Another rumor has it that this author "cannot write to save his life." This was first uttered by my high school English teacher and then followed by a long list of Stanford University English professors. The grammatical correctness of this book was due to the merciful assistance of a number of corporate public relations people on many of *The Dynamos'* staffs. They waded through the numerous misspellings and non sequiturs contained in the first draft and returned both a factually and grammatically correct copy, which was later used to prepare the final draft, and I must thank Ruth Cavin, Carolyn Cott MacPhail, and Gershon Winkler for editing it.

There are two good friends whom I want to thank not only for their help and inspiration for this book, but for their leadership in developing the formal young entrepreneurship movement in the United States. Gavin Clabaugh and Verne Harnish have spearheaded the movement to organize young entrepreneurs across America. Gavin refers to himself as a "futurist." He served as a researcher for John Naisbitt's best-selling book *Megatrends*, and is currently the founding partner of TRAC, a futures research firm in Washington, D.C., that provided the research for the *ACE 100 Top Entrepreneurs Under Thirty*. The ACE 100 was a tremendous resource for the development of this book, as was Gavin's seemingly endless supply of inspirational off-color jokes. I think it was Gavin who told me that "business is the most fun you can have with your clothes on."

Only a few years ago, Verne Harnish was a 24-year-old student at Wichita State University Graduate School of Business who would sleep on the living room floor of my California home and dream of starting an organization for college entrepreneurs. Verne stayed with me during one of his numerous trips to California when ACE (The Association of College Entrepreneurs), which he founded, was in its early stages. A number of universities, college professors, and students had tried to organize entrepreneurs on college campuses across the country. Where none before had succeeded, Verne Harnish did. Faced with a number of sarcastic unbelievers and almost no budget, Verne forged ahead and built America's largest young entrepreneurs' organization in just three years. Now there are ACE chapters on college campuses across the United States, and a special organization for graduates, the Young Entrepreneurs Organization (YEO), to which many of the dynamos belong.

The last ACE national conference, held in February 1986, in Los Angeles, was attended by 800 professors, students, and young professionals from 45 states and 12 foreign countries. There and at previous conferences, attendees have heard such speakers as former ITT chairman Harold Geneen; T. Boone Pickens, chairman of Mesa Petroleum; Arthur Lipper, founder and chairman of *Venture* magazine; and Steve Jobs, founder of Apple Computer. More information on membership in ACE or YEO can be obtained from Verne Harnish or his staff at the Association for College Entrepreneurs, Center for Entrepreneurship, Wichita State University, Wichita, Kansas 67208, phone (316) 689-3000. Along with this plug for ACE go my sincere thanks to a true friend who was a tremendous help to me in the development of this book.

I will talk about my good friend and business partner, Steve Prato, later in the book, so I won't elaborate here, except to say that Steve is a heck of a good guy to have around when you need a good kick in the pants to make things happen. Steve kicked me often. Thank you, Steve.

A special thanks to Michael Hamilton of John Wiley & Sons. He is truly one of the best business editors in the country.

Finally, having recently completed a trip throughout Eastern Europe and the Soviet Union, I must also thank our country, the United States of America. I realize it may sound a bit corny to thank one's country in the acknowledgments that introduce a book, but after visiting countries where freedom and free enterprise do not exist, I began to realize the true meaning of the statement frequently used by many authors: " . . . without which this book you are about to read would not have been possible."

B. K.

CONTENTS

WHAT IS A "DYNAMO"?

A new phenomenon is sweeping the country. While the industrialization of the United States over the preceding century and the development of Wall Street have led to a relatively well defined "old boy network," this network is seeing its influence diminish in the face of a new information-oriented, high technology society.

The emerging "new boy network" is composed of leaders in the fields of business, science, and the arts. The members of this network are achieving their objectives by traveling throughout the country and the world in search of ideas, capital, contacts, partners, and ways to turn their aspirations into reality.

The ability to tap into data bases for relevant information, the speed and ease with which travel can be accomplished, the entrepreneurial awareness developed through magazines such as *Venture* and *Inc.*, and the availability of venture capital and institutional risk capital are all factors that have brought about tremendous changes in the way business is conducted.

Leaders in business, science, and the arts compose a mobile, young society. Their lives have been greatly influenced by technology; they have attained computer literacy and developed skills that make many of their predecessors obsolete.

1

These people will be the beneficiaries of a changing social and economic environment.

There is no question that there exists today a greater opportunity than in any other decade for young people to succeed very quickly. The former path to success has become a six-lane freeway where talented young people from all backgrounds are speeding to the top. They need not be rich to get there; they need only creativity and ambition.

This book was written in recognition of the emerging business leaders who will leave their imprint on those who may follow and inspire them with their enthusiasm. We call these leaders *dynamos*.

In selecting those achievers whose stories make up the following chapters, we reviewed literally thousands of names. Many of their stories overlap. Part of this is a coincidence and part is strategic positioning. A few of the questions we put to the individuals who met our criteria were: Who is the most exciting person you know? Who is the person who is likely to have a significant impact on the business community in the near future? Whom would you be proud to have your name associated with in this book? Often they would name business associates with whom they currently work or who had helped them get started. In some cases, particularly with people in computers or real estate, the names were those of their competitors.

We put the chosen individuals through an extensive questioning: Where have you been? Where are you now? How did you get there? Where are you going? What were the greatest obstacles you had to overcome? What are the most significant factors in your success? Who were the role models who had the greatest influence on your early years? What is the best advice you can give to young entrepreneurs who aspire to build great new businesses on their ideas?

Our dynamos come from greatly varied backgrounds. Many are college dropouts; many others have advanced technical degrees and MBAs. Some are generalists who exhibit deal-making skills, some are specialists who have creatively developed a new product or process. All of them, however, have characteristics in common: ambition, drive, dedication, and self-confidence. Our dynamos are self-made. Their wealth was not inherited; success did not come to them through a family business. They are people who get new ideas in the shower and jump out and start putting them to work, instead of just drying off and forgetting them as the day goes on.

Whether dynamos are eccentrics or just highly driven achievers can be left for you to judge. It is clear, however, that much more than a desire for money or social esteem drives these dynamos toward excellence. More often than not both the drive and the satisfaction are internal. The motivation is to achieve, to lead, to change. The satisfaction lies in seeing the tangible result of work that is, not only hard, but smart. (If hard work alone led to great achievement, manual laborers would be multimillionaires.) These young millionaires or future millionaires have each found success by conceiving a clear and specific plan—a mental blueprint—and effectively articulating it to potential investors or consumers. They arrive at the plan by acting on their intuition and consciously positioning themselves for success.

This is not a how-to book, but it is one filled with secrets and lessons. If readers aspire to dynamo status, they'll find the book can accelerate the process. While individuals learn and remember most from their own mistakes, they can benefit as well from the mistakes of others. Every dynamo at one point in his or her life has been faced with some significant obstacle or failure. The failures paradoxically tended to provide the building blocks for future success and the basis for coping with future challenges.

Hard work has been a key factor in the success that the dynamos have found in their early lives, but perhaps more important, has been proper positioning. Many people are incapable of finding where their own launch pad, or starting point, lies, and they fail to plan; they fail to keep moving forward in the face of adversity. The dynamos described in the following pages have been successful, for the most part, at positioning themselves to take advantage of opportunity. While they reached their goals in a very short period, it was not because they took many shortcuts. The dynamos simply accomplish more in less time, perhaps fail more frequently and therefore learn faster.

The world of a dynamo is far from a world of certainty. What will the next 20 years hold for the dynamos described in this book? Will they be able to capitalize on past success and go on to even greater future success? Though it is unlikely that every dynamo will continue to achieve at the same rate that they have in the past, it is difficult to bet against them.

Dynamos bring a new dimension to the business environment, an element composed of confidence, lack of fear, the ability to learn from failure, and the competitive desire to win.

By using their own "new boy" network, the dynamos have been able to break down institutional barriers, thereby gaining—very early in their careers—access to large amounts of capital. They consistently look into the future; they deal with problems but don't let the barn fires along the way distract them from their objectives.

As we are business people, not psychologists, we will focus on business objectives and entrepreneurial vision as opposed to attempting to uncover subtle psychological motivation. We will leave others to hypothesize about why dynamos emerge from an otherwise average, and, at times, even mediocre society. We will let the futurists speculate on the impact that dynamos will have on changing the world around them and bringing it to a higher level of excellence.

Dynamos move at a speed that makes much of the rest of the world appear to be in slow motion, both causing and benefitting from the rapid changes taking place within society.

You may wonder why we have not included the most famous and obvious examples of young dynamos: Bill Gates of Microsoft and Mitch Kapor of Lotus; Debbi Fields of Mrs. Fields Cookies and David Liederman of David's Cookies; real estate developer Donald Trump; and, of course, the two young entrepreneurs who literally created the home computer industry, Steve Jobs and Steve Wozniak. The main reason for not including the most famous and obvious examples is because their stories are already so well known that they did not fall into the spectrum of young dynamos whom we had hoped to introduce to the public. Typically our dynamos are ages 25 to 35. Although they have proven to be great successes, they still seem to have their greatest achievements just ahead of them. We looked for the Donald Trumps and Steve Jobses of the future, people whom young professionals could identify with now because their stories represent long, hard climbs up the mountain of success without quite yet reaching the top to become "living legends." These are the people whom most young professionals will at one time or another bump into during their careers. They will see them setting out to conquer the world and wonder why they themselves are still worried about their next promotion.

By definition our dynamos are entrepreneurs, people who at an early age have decided that they are not content just to play the game, but would rather write the rules. Entrepreneurs love the independence and flexibility of being their own bosses; they use their freedom to create wealth and build their own empires rather than to lay the bricks for someone else's foundation.

Stories about the giants of the past—Carnegie, Rockefeller, Edison—will always be helpful, but we believe that our contemporaries will learn a great deal more from the stories of their peers, because their successes came out of the same conditions which many of us work under now. The boldness, tenacity, and raw ambition that they have exhibited have earned them the title of "dynamo."

FAILURE IS TO BE ANTICIPATED, NOT FEARED

*You've failed many times, although you may
   not remember.*
You fell down the first time you tried to walk.
*You almost drowned the first time you tried to
   swim, didn't you?*
*Did you hit the ball the first time you swung a
   bat?*
*Heavy hitters, the ones who hit the most home
   runs, also strike out a lot.*
*R.H. Macy failed seven times before his store
   in New York caught on.*
*English novelist John Creasey got 753 rejection
   slips before he published 564 books.*
*Babe Ruth struck out 1,330 times, but he also
   hit 714 home runs.*
Don't worry about failure.
*Worry about the chances you miss when you
   don't even try.*

(Reprinted with permission, United Technologies Corporation)

I could never understand being reluctant to do something because the fear of making a mistake is so much greater than the desire to learn or to achieve. It's hard to determine what causes a lack of confidence in an individual. Psychologists and sociologists who have been studying success for decades all have their theories about what determines a person's self-confidence, but there is no one, proven explanation. Like most personal traits, confidence is probably something instilled in early childhood. If the old saying "An apple doesn't fall very far from the tree" is true, the child of very successful and confident entrepreneurs should be the same way. However, all too often I have found the reverse to be true. In college, particularly, I saw "trust fund babies" spend the better part of their time squandering the family capital and taking illicit drugs.

Although I am not qualified to theorize about what enables an individual to have self-confidence, I know that you need self-confidence to succeed in anything, particularly as an entrepreneur. If you cannot convince yourself that you will succeed, you certainly will not convince anyone else. A belief in your own failure is a self-fulfilling prophecy. It's important for people to view failure more as a process of trial and error rather than as their ultimate doom or fate. People must make mistakes in order to learn and discover something new. It is important for us to believe that it is all right to fail. Success does not happen all the time. A society that is unwilling to take risks is one that will never grow and develop.

As we will discuss in a later chapter regarding leverage, one of the entrepreneur's major tasks is the appropriate assessment and management of risk. The other is the ability to accept failure as a learning experience, or as an obstacle along the path of success, rather than as a terrifying disaster.

If your fear of failure is greater than your desire for opportunity, you will never take the steps necessary to start your own business. Those fearful of striking out will never step up to the plate to ultimately hit the home run. At 27, Brett Davis controls a company with assets of over $5 billion, but to achieve that he had to endure and persist through a series of hair-raising setbacks and mistakes, after any one of which most people simply would have thrown in the towel. Jeff Moritz, the founder of Satcorp, took a gamble and jumped into the high stakes world of satellite communications. He made a number of bets, and although he encountered major setbacks a few times, he stayed at that table to position himself to grow with the industry.

BRETT DAVIS

BRETT DAVIS OF STOCKTON SAVINGS ASSOCIATION/TROY AND NICHOLS MORTGAGE COMPANY

What distinguishes entrepreneurs from everyone else is not their attitude toward winning but their attitude toward losing. They don't have the same fear of failure that stops others dead in their tracks. Entrepreneurs realize that failure is just part of the learning process. Davis learned his greatest lessons from his failures. "I had to concentrate not just on my loss, but on why I lost."

Less than a year after 22-year-old Brett Davis established his real estate investment company, Dadecor, Dallas Power and Light called to inform him that the electricity in his largest apartment project was about to be turned off for nonpayment. Minutes later, the phone rang again. This time it was an officer of Lone Star Gas, who informed Davis that his building was going to be "red tagged" and the gas service shut off within three days.

Davis was shocked. The manager of the complex, a close friend, had provided financial statements showing that the mortgage and expenses were being paid. He hurried over to the management office of the apartment complex, only to find that the manager had packed up in the middle of the night and moved out. Over $8 million in rent payments that had never been deposited to the company account to pay the apartment complex's bills were missing. The statements were fraudulent. He alleges that the manager had provided fraudulent financial statements which claimed the mortgage and expenses had been paid.

Faced with this $8 million horror, Brett Davis did his best to rein in a hurtling and understandable sense of fear and then concentrated on principles ingrained in him during years gone by. First among these was determination.

Brett Davis's father owned a real estate school that expanded to 21 locations over a four-state area. But the business was all but bankrupt when Brett took it over. "Only three of the school's forty teachers had been paid, the rent was two months past due on each of our twenty-one locations, the state was getting ready to revoke our license, checks were bouncing off the walls like Ping-Pong balls, the bank had lost all confidence in us, and everyone and his brother was threatening litigation."

Twelve months later, the school turned a $280,000 profit. Brett's father resumed control, and Brett was out of a job. He had, however, gained the respect and confidence of a great many local businessmen for his success in turning his father's business around. Davis used that credibility as the capital to start a company called Dadecor, through which he raised money for private limited partnerships investing in commercial real estate. It was as the president of Dadecor that Brett Davis sat down in Dallas, armed with little more than his attitude and an established acquaintance with adversity, and confronted his $8 million problem.

Filing for bankruptcy never entered his head.

What he needed was money, a lot of it, and immediately. The theft had shackled him with a $600,000-a-month ball and chain. "That," says Davis today, "was when I learned to borrow. I walked into Guaranty Bank in Oak Cliff," he remembers, "listed the properties I owned, and laid out for them what was going to happen with the utility companies the next day. Now, you'll always hear that banks will only lend you money when you don't need it, and for the most part, that's true. But Guaranty Bank gave me a million dollar signature loan that day. And I'll never forget it."

Davis paid off the utilities, but that was only dodging the first bullet. He had to find money to make the units habitable once more, pay a newly hired management company, and meet mortgage payments on the original notes. Soon after, Davis closed a real estate deal that netted him $4.5 million. "I got to keep it for thirty days," he recalls. "And then that great black hole swallowed it up."

The crisis went on for months. During it, Davis started work at seven each morning and rarely finished before two or three the next morning. "Occasionally," he says with a grin, "it would be four or five in the morning, and when I got up to go home, my seat cushion would come up with me. That's when I knew things were *really* bad."

Things got so bad that Brett couldn't pay his office staff and his wife Laurie couldn't pay the doctor bills for the birth of their child, one of five that they have now. Laurie had to take the phone off the hook at night and Brett had to work from 7 A.M. to 1 A.M. every day. During that time, on the first Tuesday of each month, Davis had to show up at the courthouse steps to protect his property from foreclosure. "I sat at home every night just thinking about how I would survive the next day. At the office I always had to give the impression that I was too busy to pay the bills rather than allow people to know I didn't have the money, which would cause my creditors and employees to panic."

He forced himself to maintain an appearance of calm and confidence, with his own staff and with his creditors. "If you're one of these guys who gets superexcited over something," he says, "everybody reacts that way. Then, when there's a problem, bankers start closing the lines and employees start looking for other jobs. Believe me, it can all come to an end really quickly when everyone gets nervous."

But Davis did not give up, and no matter how tough things got he never lost the support of his wife and family. Through a series of refinancings and profitable deal developments, Davis turned back the tide of adversities. "Adversity and I have become good friends," says Davis. In fact, Davis has proved that he thrives on adversity. He not only was able to turn around a situation that would have spelled disaster for most other people, but he used the lessons he learned from this experience to build one of the largest real estate holding and financial conglomerates owned by an individual under thirty in the United States and possibly in the world. At twenty-seven, Davis presides over an empire that grosses over $750 million in annual revenues and services over $5 billion in assets.

Five years later, Davis is still paying $80,000 a month on the final obligations of the debt incurred from his "friend's" theft. He has prospered, he insists, not so much in spite of the adversities he experienced but because of them. Nietzsche wrote: "What doesn't destroy me makes me stronger," and no one proves the truth of that better than Brett Davis.

Davis's holdings are diverse. In 1983, he acquired First Savings and Loan of Fort Stockton, a small west Texas institution with a negative net worth. Today, renamed Stockton Savings Association, the company has a positive net worth, and has posted annual revenues of $75 million, and operates from an asset base of $750 million.

Troy and Nichols Mortgage Company, based in Monroe, Louisiana, is a wholly owned subsidiary reporting $650 million in revenues and serving over $4 billion in single-family residential loans. It is the fourth largest privately held mortgage company in the United States, and the nation's twelfth largest issuer of Ginnie Mae securities. Troy and Nichols employs more than 650 people throughout its 38 offices. Dadecor, Davis's first company, is a real estate firm with $20 million in revenues. He also owns Four Seasons Travel, First Fidelity Financial, Delco Insurance, and a 50 percent stake in Poole Mortgage of Oklahoma. What makes Brett Davis's portfolio of businesses so remarkable is that he had assembled it by the time he was 25 years old, and without a penny of inherited wealth behind him. His achievement is one of the most inspiring stories of modern American business.

Davis insists, "What distinguishes the entrepreneur from everyone else is not his attitude toward winning but toward losing. Entrepreneurs are not afraid of failure. They understand it to be an essential element of the learning process necessary to succeed. Most important, they know that no one else is in a position to tell them they have failed. They fail only when they themselves have given up. We are each master of our own fate."

Davis believes that deep down most people would like to work for themselves but are afraid to. "I therefore think it unfortunate, but true," he says, "that other people often need you to fail in order to justify their own fears and inertia."

For him, however, "Risk is the lifeblood of enterprise." And taking risks has yielded the most valuable lessons of his business life.

In 1983, at around the same time he was negotiating the purchase of First Savings and Loan of Fort Stockton, Davis heard that Stockton, Watley, Daven & Company (SWD), a Florida mortgage company, was for sale. He applied to Morgan Stanley, the investment bankers handling the sale, for an offering memorandum. They refused to send him one. Morgan Stanley could not believe that a 24-year-old high school dropout was a serious buyer. He then contacted a host of other investment bankers to represent him. No one would. Eventually, Davis sent Morgan Stanley his financial statement, and they supplied him with an offering memorandum. He was the only potential bidder out of an interested field of 180 who was not an institution.

From the initial bids, Morgan Stanley intended to narrow the field to 15. Davis was willing to bid more than the other bidders because his main interest was the real estate that SWD owned, which he felt was worth more than the amount being carried on the company's books. "Now, I figured most people would just look at the value of the servicing portfolio," says Davis, "and bid around 2 percent, or eighty million dollars, so to get anybody's attention, I'd have to go higher than that. So I bid a hundred million. Well, it worked, and I made the first cut. So now I was one of fifteen, and what do you know but all those investment bankers who only two weeks before had wanted nothing to do with me are suddenly calling me at all hours trying to get my business. I went with Paine Webber."

Morgan Stanley then sent out a much thicker dossier on SWD. Davis discovered that SWD's real estate department was even bigger than the mortgage operation, and it owned real estate all over Florida. After visiting the company to do his due diligence, Davis submitted a second bid that would decide the final three bidders. This time he upped the ante to $155 million. He made it to the final three, "along with two other small-time bidders," he laughs, "called First Bank of Boston and Shearson/American Express. It was a real joke."

By this time, Davis was into the deal for about $400,000, half of which Paine Webber had demanded up front. He then went back to Florida for the second round of due diligence. "And I have an army of lawyers and accountants going through the company books, department by department," he says, "each clicking away at a hundred to a hundred and fifty dollars an hour, as well as their air fares and room and board."

Along with the final bid, Davis and his competitors were obliged to submit proof of financing. He went to three north Texas banks. "They turned me down flat," he says. Brett's situation was further complicated by his concurrent efforts to get state approval for the purchase of First Savings and Loan of Fort Stockton. He told the state board of his plans for SWD. They refused him permission to buy the savings and loan, so Davis found a partner for the SWD deal. Still the state refused. Davis found a third partner and secured additional funding from a fourth. The state gave its consent.

As far as Davis was concerned, however, finding the cash was a purely academic matter. As he explains it: "My intention all along was to pay for the mortgage company by using its own escrow accounts. In other words, to make it an almost totally leveraged buy-out. You see, the conventional wisdom then existing with regard to monies held in escrow by savings and loans was that the FSLIC insurance, with its ceiling of $100,000 per account, left the greater part of the escrow funds uninsured. My attorneys, though, had rendered an opinion that since the monies were held in escrow for each individual's or family's mortgage, then they were separately insured, and thus all covered by the FSLIC. So, while I had to prove I had financing of one hundred fifty-five million, the same day we closed I knew we could immediately arrange to have the one hundred-twenty million dollars that SWD held in escrow accounts transferred straight into the accounts of Stockton and my two savings and loan partners. My strategy meant that we only had to provide thirty million of our own dollars, and that was no problem. To our knowledge, it had never been done before, but we reckoned it was absolutely flawless."

Davis' final bid was for $160 million.

Throughout the dealings, Phillips Petroleum, the seller, had told everyone, and had written the statement into the offering memorandum, that they would not sell SWD in parts, for in addition to mortgage and real estate, SWD also dealt in insurance. "And that," says Davis, "is where we figured we had it made, because neither of the other bidders were really interested in the entire company, only in certain parts. Nor were they legally entitled to own SWD's insurance subsidiary. First Boston couldn't because insurance is classified as commerce, in which banks are forbidden to engage, and American Express because of certain antitrust regulations. We believed we were the only remaining bidder legally allowed to own SWD. There was no way we could lose."

They did.

Contrary to the offering memorandum and their previous statements, Phillips sold the mortgage company to First Bank of Boston and the real estate to an independent supplier of theirs who later sold the properties at a substantial profit.

Davis describes it as "the bleakest, blackest day I remember." He and his partners were convinced they had won. Sources inside SWD had told them that the $160 million was the highest bid, and the company's senior management had even started the business of currying favor with the men they were convinced were to be their new bosses. To this day, Davis believes that his investment bankers suspected from the start that there was no way Phillips was going to sell him the company. He felt "they all just used me to keep upping the price because my bids were consistently higher than the others." He stated, "It was so tough to swallow. All of a sudden, I felt like a naive twenty-four-year-old who's just been played like a drum." He has since been known to refer to investment bankers as among the finest specimens of the oldest profession.

Looking back at what then seemed like a catastrophe, Davis says, "Nobody would have blamed me if I'd cut my losses and run. I'd tried to play in the big leagues, and I'd got whipped."

Far from quitting, Brett Davis went after another mortgage company less than four months later.

His experience with SWD served him well.

This time, Davis had beaten out all the other bidders for the Troy and Nichols Mortgage Company. This time, he had E. F. Hutton on his side.

Davis and his lawyers, along with the sellers and their lawyers, arrived in E. F. Hutton's New York attorney's office for the closing. In Davis's own words: "The total purchase price was $60 million, split up as $50 million for the stock and $10 million for the servicing. For tax reasons, I wanted to pay less for the stock and more for the servicing, which meant that we paid the same price in the end. E. F. Hutton's commission, however, was based on the purchase price of the stock, not the servicing, so when I brought up what we wanted to do they got really agitated and threatened to put a stop to the negotiations right there and then. When that happened, one of the sellers jumped up and said, 'I don't see why we're paying you a three-million-dollar commission to put up with this sort of crap!' My lawyer said, 'You mean *you're* paying them a commission, too!' And he immediately threatened E. F. Hutton with a lawsuit for taking commissions from both sides undisclosed, but did not press the claim."

Davis shakes his head and says: "That was when I first heard the saying 'When E. F. Hutton talks, the FBI listens.' And then I put my hands together and said to myself, 'Thank you, Paine Webber,' because having been rolled by *them* a few months earlier I had no intention of letting the lesson go to waste."

Davis's attorney turned to the senior seller's attorney and asked him if the sales split was agreeable. The seller said yes. Davis said, "Do you want to sell me your company?"

Again the seller said yes. "Fine," said Brett, "then why don't you, me, and our lawyers go back to the hotel and settle this thing ourselves."

And that was exactly what they did, leaving the E. F. Hutton people, as Davis remembers it, "sitting around their huge conference table looking like some orthodontist had just wired their mouths open." Both Davis and the seller later agreed to pay E. F. Hutton a commission on the deal but at a substantially reduced rate.

Anyone meeting Brett Davis in the street would not realize that they were talking to a dynamo. Shy to the point of embarrassment, soft-spoken, and waging a constant war against weight, he is a man whose strength derives exclusively from his values. Because of the circumstances of his own childhood, he is a family man before he is anything. His best friend and his greatest resource is his wife. His greatest comfort is their five children. Davis, a Mormon, often recalls Mormon past president David O. McKay's statement that "no success justifies failure in the home."

One final incident is most revealing of Brett Davis's character. In 1985, he was asked to speak at Brigham Young University, the school that had once refused to accept him as a student because he did not have a high school diploma. In the filled auditorium that day sat a man who had been one of the investors in the limited partnerships that owned the Dallas apartments. As part of the speech, Davis recounted his troubles over the $8 million theft. Immediately after the talk, the investor came up to Davis and said, "I never knew." Brett Davis had never told any of his investors. He had just kept paying them each month, right out of his own twenty-two-year-old pocket.

Perhaps T. Boone Pickens and Marvin Davis better start looking over their shoulders.

JEFF MORITZ

JEFF MORITZ
OF SATCORP

"Be willing to make mistakes and even fail. Even though failure is not part of my everyday thought process, the experience of failure is critical to understanding success."

"I got a BA in liberal arts at St. Bonaventure University, located between several large snowdrifts in upstate New York. After graduating from Hofstra Law School, I practiced law for six weeks before I realized that I had no real desire to be a lawyer," says entertainment and satellite entrepreneur Jeff Moritz. Moritz, now 37, shrewdly parlayed his legal education and a nose for opportunity into a minicommunications conglomerate.

After law school Moritz cut his teeth in the entertainment business by organizing a specialized marketing company called Classic Sports, which became a subsidiary of Telephone Marketing Programs (TMP). This venture created and produced national sports events as a medium for sponsors such as Converse, BMW, and Miller Beer. In 1980, Classic Sports grossed more than $2 million and was developing nicely when Andy McKelvey, the CEO of TMP, circulated a newspaper article that changed Moritz's career path. The article described the Federal Communications Commission's decision to deregulate communications in the United States. McKelvey noted that historically deregulation has resulted in new opportunities emerging in the industry involved and encouraged Moritz to explore the consequences of this particular deregulation.

Moritz's study identified satellite communications as the area most likely to explode once free competition and open skies became in fact the operative market forces. The study concluded that (1) if private individuals could own unlicensed satellite antennae, anyone who owned many antennae, owned a network in theory; (2) the likely emergence of new networks would create a demand for more satellite capacity; and (3) fast moving management groups could take positions if they could accurately anticipate the evolving niches.

His strategy for filling these niches entailed enrolling new executives, new relationships, and new investors. Moritz began to focus on the first niche conclusion: to launch a new network by controlling, owning, and operating a national network of satellite antennae in targeted markets. He was determined that the placement of each dish be the result of a partnership relationship with top U.S. colleges and universities, and in 1981 Campus Entertainment Network was organized. It licensed various giant events, ranging from Ali vs. Holmes (on two campuses) to the final Who concert (40 locations) to a production of *Sophisticated Ladies* (16 locations). "In retrospect, this plan approached lunacy in terms of naked ambition," admitted Moritz, "and probably had to fail, since it represented fundamental changes in a number of established industries." Each event encountered industry resistance plus the mistakes that plague any new project.

Moritz, in purchasing the rights to show Ali's last fight in the state of Florida, could not rent any of the giant indoor arenas in Miami, the state's largest city, for the closed circuit event. He rolled the dice and contracted for the Orange Bowl, an outdoor arena, in the middle of hurricane season! He considered purchasing rain insurance (until he computed his projected premium).

In the center of the Orange Bowl he built a screen 60 feet by 120 feet, from plywood and metal scaffolding and weighing more than 18 tons. It was completed just six hours before the event. Moritz talked Muhammed Ali into making dozens of personalized radio spots complete with adlibbed original poetry for each of Moritz's markets. The event was coming together.

As if on cue, disaster reared its predictable head. Hurricane alerts flashed over weather reports in Miami 24 hours before the event. It began to look as though this 18-ton screen was built in the wrong place. Only 5,000 tickets had been sold and the screen location meant that the 120-foot-long screen would have a 10-foot picture. But the hand of providence intervened and while the giant projector was hoisted into the stands, the sun broke through the clouds. More than

18,000 tickets were sold on the day of the event for $20, $50, and $100, breaking the all-time Orange Bowl record for walk-up business.

During this time, Moritz met a wide range of fellow entrepreneurs who would play different roles in this odyssey. One, Clifford Friedland, brought him a deal that filled the second niche: the anticipated demand for more satellite capacity. Friedland was busily engaged in launching a cable tv channel featuring music videos, and he proposed a true wildcatter's venture—to launch their own satellite.

Many new companies are founded by partnership between a dreamer and a business person, one person creates the idea and the other carries it out. Moritz was certainly the businessman, and Friedland was never to be accused of being short on dreams. Friedland spent months studying the government's bidding system for the auction of satellite transponder slots prior to scheduled NASA launches, and he realized that almost anyone could initiate a bid for a satellite and a transponder that could give them the ability to broadcast across a section of the United States. Friedland approached Moritz with the idea of establishing their own satellite company so they could control broadcasts of their videos over their own cable networks.

"At first I thought he was nuts," says Moritz of Friedland's new idea, "but when I listened, I realized he was right." Under the deregulation policies of the satellite industry, common carriers allowed anyone to apply for transponders on a first-come, first-served basis. Friedland decided to submit his name for all the satellite launches scheduled for the next decade and later found himself being placed on the list for 17 satellite transponders—more transponders than any one person or company had in the United States at that time.

"Here was Clifford sitting with the rights to seventeen satellite transponders," Moritz says, "a guy who previously made his living as a designer of men's underwear and who had a current net worth of twelve dollars." Although getting the rights to 17 transponders proved to be one accomplishment, closing on the acquisition of a full satellite would prove to be quite another task. A small obstacle stood in Friedland's way—the few million dollars that were required to close officially on the satellite transponders. A few *hundred* million dollars were required to own his own license and satellite.

Undaunted by their lack of capital, Friedland and Moritz set up a third company, United States Satellite Systems, Inc. (USSSI), dedicated to the development of their plan. Moritz approached the task of raising money with characteristic fervor. He tried to find it by calling everyone he knew who had it. His only problem was that no one he knew happened to have a few million in high-risk capital lying around.

Moritz then asked a friend to go through the phone book and call all the big accounting and law firms in town to try to get a referral. Their determination paid off. They were put in contact with Laurent Gerschel, the grandson of, and heir to, the world's greatest investment banker, André Meyer of Lazard Frères. Meyer had amassed a fortune on Wall Street by helping create and finance corporations like Avis, Holiday Inn, and ITT. Gerschel, a medical doctor with a hereditary instinct for deal making, realized the potential of Moritz and Friedland's project and agreed to back them.

According to Moritz, Gerschel saw the satellite project as being like a real estate deal. He analyzed the demand for the property—the transponders and their designated broadcasting rights and capabilities—and determined the value of tying up the rights and selling or leasing them back to big companies who needed the transponders. In addition, Gerschel and Moritz developed plans to use a few of the transponders for their own projects.

The main player in the satellite game at the time was a company called Satellite Business Systems (SBS) which was a partnership that included IBM, Aetna Life Insurance, and COMSAT. According to Moritz, "We wanted to position USSSI to become to SBS what Pepsi is to Coke, but to do this we needed a strong partner." So Moritz went partner hunting and bagged Wang and Control Data Corporation (CDC).

Wang's and CDC's interests in joining the partnerships were their desire to build the office systems of the future and their need for satellite capacity to interconnect the components of those systems.

After a number of discussions, USSSI sent proposals to both Wang and CDC. Moritz describes the experience: "We had an employee who, after a three-martini lunch, sent CDC's proposal to Wang and Wang's to CDC." This put the heat on Wang who then realized they were bidding against CDC. The mistake encouraged Wang to seal the deal right away. "When we closed the deal, we reflected on how this all happened," recollects Moritz. "We came home, gave our secretary a bonus, and considered naming her VP of Strategic Planning."

Wang joined USSSI as a partner in November 1982 and committed $5 million in investments for just under 10 percent of the company. USSSI put the second step of its plan into action. Moritz worked with his partners to bring on Bob Hall, who was the chairman and CEO of his greatest competitor, SBS, as chairman and CEO of USSSI. Hall put together a team of the industry's best engineers to work on developing advanced technological applications for their satellite resources.

As the satellite launch dates drew near, USSSI was required to demonstrate a $300 million capitalization in order to obtain final FCC approval for its license. To raise that capital, Moritz and Hall realized that they would have to sell out all of the capacity on both of their satellites. They approached Federal Express Corporation, which needed special satellites for its new "ZAP Mail" service. A deal was proposed where Federal Express would agree to sign a $295 million lease and thereby meet the FCC capitalization requirements for all of the capacity on two satellites. The negotiations between USSSI and Federal Express were intense and drawn out. Meanwhile time was running short until the FCC deadline. According to Moritz, "The deal was finally struck at six P.M., July 20, 1984, just six hours before the FCC withdrew its license due to lack of proof of capitalization."

With the closing of the final contract, USSSI seemed firmly secure in its bid to acquire its final license. With Bob Hall at the helm of USSSI, Moritz and Gerschel decided to become partners in an investment company named Satcorp, Inc. which would invest in satellite businesses and high technology video research and development (R&D) projects.

Their first deal was to acquire the assets of Campus Entertainment Network, rename it Campus Network, Inc., and fund it with $10 million, with a combination of internal funds. For subsequent funding, they set up a limited partnership that offered investors an equity percentage after they received a two-for-one payout. In addition, the limited partners received all the tax benefits.

The plan for Campus Network involved using high powered satellite transponders, which would cover the whole United States, and extra large (3.75 meters) permanent dishes to pick up the weak signals of wide beam transmission. They targeted their service to provide a full range of television fare to the top 500 colleges.

Today Campus Network has contracts with 150 colleges, including Ohio State, MIT, and Brigham Young University. More than 2 million students on campus can watch Campus Network each week. Another 4 million cable homes each week can watch its mix of music, comedy, news, and educational programs. Campus Network also builds giant videocenters with high-definition television screens at selected schools. Twenty-three facilities have been completed to date. Using its network of videocenters, on March 1, 1985, Campus Network had the first ever transmission of a motion picture by satellite to a giant screen in a digital audio format. This technological breakthrough was made possible by the R&D investments by Satcorp—and will ultimately be exploited by still another to-be-named Satcorp subsidiary.

While Campus Network and Satcorp have been extremely successful, the fortunes of USSSI took an unexpected turn in 1985. The board of Federal Express refused to ratify its contract six months after it was signed—and long after USSSI modified its system for ZAP Mail. Federal Express recently announced the discontinuation of its ZAP mail service in which it took a write-off in excess of $100 million. This catastrophic turn of events dampened the success of Satcorp and according to Moritz provided him with an invaluable lesson as an entrepreneur. "If you are an entrepreneur, don't take yourself out too early; anticipate that things may go wrong." The saga of USSSI is not over, Moritz and Satcorp acquired the rights to all of the assets of USSSI in late 1985—and it may well rise again.

Moritz sees himself as a futurist. He believes the greatest way to make money lies in analyzing future trends in society and industry and participating early in the development. Moritz calls Toffler's *The Third Wave* the most significant book ever written for futurist-entrepreneurs. Moritz was so impressed with the book that he called Toffler and arranged a meeting that was to last two days. Moritz said the book and the subsequent meeting taught him how to plan in the context of future change. Moritz envisions Satcorp as someday becoming a merchant bank of the satellite and telecommunications industry.

"Ten years ago it was unpopular in business to be young, aggressive, and purposeful," says Moritz. "Now the Yuppies between twenty-five and forty are the decision makers who make things happen." Moritz further defines the rapid changes in society and their impact on people by pointing out, "Today, there is even a big difference between the ages of twenty-five and thirty. People twenty-five years old have used personal computers in college, many people thirty years old haven't. PCs will eventually dominate the world of business and the computer generation will be the haves; the rest will be the have nots."

When asked what advice he could give to other entrepreneurs interested in entering his industry, Moritz responds, "In general, be willing to make mistakes and even fail. Even though failure is not part of my everyday thought process, the experience of failure is critical to understanding success.

"I'm not going to tell you how to do it, because I have the horses and I'm going to get to the finish line first," says Moritz, "but this industry is the only one I have ever seen where you can begin at the top."

YOU HAVE TO HAVE BIG DREAMS AND CLEAR VISION

Is the American dream still alive and well? Is it still realistic for a poor man to dream of making it big, of becoming rich in America today? Ask that question of Raphael Collado and Ramon Morales, two men who grew up in America's most notorious slums, the South Bronx and East Harlem, and who later returned to their old neighborhoods to build a successful high tech company which in 1986 grossed over $7 million in sales and projected $10 million for 1987.

Brett Davis, whom we read about earlier, has often said: "It is an entrepreneur's divine right to dream." Dreams are just the very beginning of the creation of new realities, just as an idea is the first step in developing a new product or service. Without dreams or ideas there would be no great achievements, no innovations, no great works of arts, no novels, no new fashions, and probably no fun.

But as dynamos Collado and Morales will tell you, simply to dream is not enough. You have to have a clear vision of both your goal and how you want to get there. As you will learn from the following chapters, Protocom Devices was founded on a tremendous amount of idealism; the partners

wanted to provide leadership and jobs for the underprivileged
in their community while they were making money for themselves. However, building a successful company requires much
more than ideals alone. Their firm commitment to their ideals,
combined with their hard-nosed determination to succeed,
made Protocom much more than their childhood dream. It
made it a profitable high-growth company.

RAPHAEL COLLADO AND RAMON MORALES

RAPHAEL COLLADO AND RAMON MORALES OF PROTOCOM DEVICES

The key to their success is believing in their dream and "empowering other people to succeed and believe in their ability to make a difference. We want to show people how to take control of their lives by becoming financially independent."

Raphael Collado loosens his tie as he emerges from his temporary office building on Willow Avenue in the heart of the South Bronx. Squinting against the hot summer sun, he surveys the area. "You know, I was born less than a block from here," Collado says. Burned buildings can be seen in the distance, relics of the economic blight and neglect that for decades have made the South Bronx the most notorious slum in the United States. "The few of us that were able to make it out of here swore that we would come back to help," says Collado. "Not everyone came back. Some enjoyed the good life too much, but we're here and we're going to show you what we are doing to bring the South Bronx back to life."

The 32-year-old chairman and CEO of Protocom Devices has to go off to a sales meeting, but he leaves me in good hands. My designated tour guide is Ramon Morales, 33, Protocom's president. Pepo, the company's manufacturing manager, came along to join us for the trip to the company's new manufacturing facility, still under construction.

Collado is black; Morales and Pepo are Puerto Rican immigrants. Morales grew up close to Collado in nearby East Harlem. They attended school together at Monsignor William R. Kelly Junior High School, a New York Catholic school that offered academic opportunities to gifted underprivileged minority students. Financial problems later forced the school to close, and both Collado and Morales swore to reopen it.

Pepo is a recent immigrant. Both he and Morales are proud of their Hispanic heritage—I can feel that pride as they talk about the company's achievements and their contributions to the community. "Before we take you to our new manufacturing facility, let us show you around the South Bronx. We want to show you both the good and the bad. Now let's start with the bad," Morales says.

"Sorry, no BMW," Morales jokes. His car is a 1984 Toyota, not the sort of car you would expect the president of a successful high tech company to drive. Within minutes we are passing row after row of abandoned buildings. All have smashed windows and interiors gutted by fire. Some are reduced to piles of rubble.

I had seen these buildings before, not just here, but throughout other blighted sections of New York, the areas that tourists never see and most city dwellers take great pains to avoid. Areas like Harlem and the Bedford Stuyvesant section of Brooklyn. Areas that the glamour and riches of the mainstream New York society never touched or chose to ignore. Areas where, between the ages of 12 to 15, I used to ride through every summer on my father's truck to deliver mattresses to the small retail stores that dotted these areas and provided furnishings on extended credit terms.

All those blighted areas looked bad, but somehow they couldn't rival the chilling deprivation in the South Bronx. It looks like bombed-out sections of Berlin at the end of World War II. My father made sure that I went on deliveries to these areas so I would learn about the "real world" at an early age. My experiences there included dodging muggers who tried to steal our cash delivery receipts and encountering gangs so brazen, or perhaps desperate, that they would try to break open the back doors of the truck with a crowbar while we were still moving in traffic.

"This was for far too long the legacy of the South Bronx," says Morales. "Come, let us show you the future." We drive a few blocks and Morales points to an area filled with dozens of new single-family homes. If it hadn't been for what I'd just seen less than half a mile away, I could have believed I was back in suburbia. Adjacent to these homes are vacant lots, which were previously covered with the rubble of burned-out tenements. Now new single-family homes had been built on those lots. "You wouldn't believe how property values have risen around here. A few years ago the owners would rather have burned their places down than try to sell them. Now, like in some areas of Harlem, the land is being reclaimed by young professional families, some of whom take a 10-minute commute to the city," Morales tells me.

Within minutes we park outside Protocom's new 40,000-square-foot corporate headquarters and manufacturing facility at Bathgate, the South Bronx's new technology park, which was financed by New York's Port Authority. "Can you believe it, a high technology industrial park right in the heart of the South Bronx?" Morales says with a smile. Pepo and Morales quickly guide me through the front door. There we are met by a Puerto Rican security guard, who smiles and greets Pepo and Morales in Spanish. This is definitely the most enthusiastic security guard in the United States. He can't do enough for his new employers who, like him, grew up in the area and shared the same ethnic background. It's clear to me that the founders of Protocom instill real pride in their employees, who until now were not used to seeing black and Hispanic employers in the area. They are living proof that there is hope. You can see it in the security guard's eyes.

Morales leads the tour of the offices but turns over the lead to Pepo as we enter the manufacturing area. This is Pepo's domain, and Morales's actions demonstrate that he is a true believer in delegating authority. Pepo and his staff worked with the industry's top consultants to design the factory floor plan for maximum efficiency. "If we are serious about keeping manufacturing jobs here in the United States, and particularly in this community, we can't afford to be second best. We had to plan to develop the most efficient manufacturing facility per square foot," says Pepo. We talk about everything from just-in-time delivery systems to open manufacturing floorplans that allow for production line flexibility. It's clear that these young entrepreneurs are not ordinary idealists dreaming of great social programs. They are deadly serious business people with a realistic and determined plan for achieving their goals. "Make no mistake about it," says Morales, "the bottom line is still profits. No profits, no jobs; no jobs, no pride. . . . We don't want people pointing their fingers at us in the future and saying, 'Those guys may have meant well but they were just another minority-run business that couldn't make it on their own!' "

Protocom started its operations in early 1983 in the apartment of a co-worker of Collado's, Charles Gallucci. Collado had Gallucci and William Josuna, both friends, co-workers, and engineers, to help him design and produce a "protocol conversion device" or PAD (Pocket Assembler/Disassembler), which would allow communication between different makes and models of computers even if they did not use similar programming languages. Collado and his partners' focus was on creating an inexpensive networking device that would allow companies with differing computer systems in their various offices around the country to communicate easily without having to replace their expensive existing computer systems. Collado saw the need for the product while working as an engineer for a number of large companies, but since the initial market seemed too small to justify his employer's interest, Collado decided to go in on his own.

With capital of $10,000, loaned to them by their attorneys, the three engineers slaved away without salary in Gallucci's apartment, hoping to develop their product before their money ran out. Less than two years later, Protocom now employs 28 people and has an annual sales volume of over $7 million. It has developed specialized PAD compatibility enhancement for large computer systems that allow those made by Sperry, Burroughs, Honeywell, Hewlett-Packard, Digital Equipment Corporation, IBM, and others to communicate in X-25 packet switching networks. The X-25 network has increasingly become the favored networking system both in the United States and abroad. "Packet switching," the communications process where streams of information are broken down into small packets that are transmitted individually, is far more efficient and cost-effective than maintaining a permanently open leased line for data communications. Protocom's PAD can assemble outgoing information in one computer language and disassemble incoming information in another, now allowing two computer systems that previously couldn't communicate to work together in the same communications network. If you saw the movie *War Games*, you got a taste for how easy (and how dangerous) it is to break into some data networks. Protocom's system comes as close to being 100 percent secure as can be imagined with today's data communications technology, and that serves as an additional advantage.

Protocom's P2500 PAD lists for $9,500. About the size of a large hardcover book, it can be used by as many as 40 computer terminals simultaneously. Most customers buy the PADs in quantity to support the functioning of large computer systems. Typical Protocom customers include companies like Boeing Computer Systems, which has ordered $1.5 million worth of PADs for a network it is building for the state government of Pennsylvania, and the Paradyne Corporation, which has ordered $600,000 worth for the construction of a banking network linking a bank in one state, whose operations are based on Burroughs computers, with a bank recently acquired in another state, whose equipment is based on Sperry.

Collado, who has worked for ITT Corporation's Courier division, GTE Corporation's Telenet division, and as a senior product manager for Timeplex, Inc., realized that as the company grew beyond Gallucci's apartment, they would need to add management and organizational talent to their already strong engineering expertise. He turned to his childhood friend, Ramon Morales. After they had both left the Monsignor Kelly school, Collado pursued his engineering career at Brooklyn's Polytechnic Institute while Morales studied sociology and economics at Harvard. After graduation Morales worked at Prudential Insurance Company developing computer-based warehouse operations, but soon left to do social and consulting work for various city and state agencies. Collado knew that in Morales he would find both the organizational leadership abilities the company needed and the shared social commitment to improving the South Bronx that he demanded in order to achieve his noncorporate goals.

Collado succeeded in luring away Morales from his present job with a $367-a-month salary and the promise of fulfilling a dream. But Morales is quick to point out that it was just not the founders who endured the hardships required for their later success. "During the shoestring times of our startup phase, everyone from engineers to secretaries went three months without pay, but no one left the company. They believed in Protocom and knew that Protocom believed in them."

Collado recalls the advice he received from one venture capitalist when he informed him of his decision to locate the company in the South Bronx: "You move a good thing into shit, it will turn into shit." Most other venture capitalists agreed. Collado decided to say no to the venture capitalists because "we wanted to maintain equity control so we could maintain our vision. If we were going to fail, we wanted to fail on our own business plan. After all, that is what entrepreneurship is all about, independence, hard work, and a vision." Collado was convinced that compromising their vision of the company would destroy their motivation and the meaningfulness of their achievement, and besides, "The rent here is cheap." Morales agreed, and tenaciously pursued turning an issue that was providing a big negative to their financing opportunities into a positive.

Morales decided to sell their desire to locate and create jobs in the South Bronx as an asset rather than a liability. He quickly found a buyer, the Port Authority of New York and New Jersey. The Port Authority was already involved in developing the Bathgate Industrial Park in the South Bronx, in the hopes that the rejuvenation of the area would lead to more employment and higher land values. Morales convinced the Port Authority that Protocom represented an excellent future growth-oriented tenant that would also create more jobs for the community. The Port Authority researched the business and the founders' backgrounds. They were impressed and agreed to provide $4.4 million in loans to purchase equipment and construct a 40,000-square-foot factory—space enough to enable them to increase production more than eightfold. Protocom ultimately received far better terms than any other venture capitalist would have provided by sticking to its vision and ideals. It did not have to give up any equity.

The Port Authority deal really paid off for the founders when it was time for the firm to go public. Both were able to retain fairly high equity stakes in the company after the public offering, which raised $4.6 million in capital. Their holdings are valued at over $3 million, but more important, they still retain the control necessary to maintain their dream and continue with their vision.

After the offering, a jubilant Collado was often seen handing out his personal shares to employees in the hallway. The real advantage to their newly acquired wealth, however, was that they were able to keep their promise to their childhood teacher, Brother Brian Carty, to help reopen the school for bright underprivileged minority children. Recently Protocom pledged $50,000 for the project, now called the De La Salle Academy, and it continues to aid and support the school by providing computer equipment and offering tours of the factory to show the kids living proof that they can hope to succeed.

Morales maintains that the key to their success is believing in their dream and "empowering other people to succeed and believe in their ability to make a difference." Morales constantly uses the term "empowering" when referring to what he believes his management philosophy and corporate culture does for his employees. Empowering people is the process of helping them believe in their goals and in their ability to achieve those goals. Particularly in areas like the South Bronx, where the people are poor, empowering takes on a political as well as a business message. "We want to empower people to make them independent of political forces that would simply seek to exploit them. We want to show them how to take control of their lives by becoming financially independent of the public dole," says Collado. "We believe we will succeed and our employees believe we will succeed. That is why Protocom will be a $150 million company within five years," adds Morales. "In the old days, products were dug out of the earth or drilled or fashioned, the products were external to them. Today products are more a direct result of people. You have to be able to address the people in business because they are more a part of the product today—you're dealing more with people and creativity now. Our people believe in what they are doing. That's why we create great products. If your people don't get along together, sooner or later your end product will look like shit.

"In a nutshell," he continues, "what Protocom is all about is showing people, particularly in communities like this one, that they can participate in controlling their own destiny and take part in the growth opportunities of the future through entrepreneurship." Protocom's owners want to prove that people will do a good job if given the chance and that the poor communities should not be deprived of a chance at the more meaningful jobs offered by the technological revolution. They believe this can be truly accomplished only through entrepreneurship, and not with public grants.

Protocom's vision was never demonstrated more clearly than in a recent NBC documentary, "To the South Bronx With Love," in which the hosts interviewed one of the Protocom employees, Eddie Garcia. Eddie grew up in the South Bronx. He told how he had joined the company in an unskilled staff position and then was encouraged to take classes so he could move up into a technical position. Then, with tears in his eyes, he told the reporters how he was now able to go home to his children at night and say to them with pride, "Your daddy works in an office with computers," rather than having to say he cleans toilets in a nursing home.

Not long ago, the New York politicos launched a now notorious campaign, spending over $1 million to put pretty decals of picture windows with flower pots over the boarded-up windows of abandoned South Bronx buildings so that the area would look more appealing from the highway. Politicians' covering over the problems of communities like the South Bronx won't work. Entrepreneurs like Collado and Morales will.

"There are too many pseudo-entrepreneurs today," says Collado. "They want the BMW and the big house, come up with some scam and take it public in three years. But that's not what it's about. . . . We've got a task to do. We're trying to build a Silicon Valley in the South Bronx. Not everybody here is out lighting fires and stealing transistor radios. Every company wants to make good products and be profitable. Being young entrepreneurs, we're downright fanatical about both those goals. But at Protocom, we have another goal as well. We are zealously proud of what we have done technologically and we want to do no less socially. The American dream lives in the South Bronx, as it does everywhere, and we hope we can help make it a reality for more of the community."

"DON'T TAKE 'NO' FOR AN ANSWER"

"No." For centuries, that word has dashed hopes and killed prospects. But for some people, "no" does not mean an end of the project or an end to their dreams for success, for them "no" simply means "Try again."

You can learn a lot from a person by the way he or she responds to a "no." As you will see, one important characteristic that makes the dynamos rise above the crowd is their ability to overcome rejection, their unwillingness to take no for an answer. Had Edison been willing to accept failure after his first few dozen tries, we would not have had the lightbulb; had a then unknown author not persisted, after numerous rejections from Hollywood producers and New York publishers, we would not have had the pleasure of experiencing the classic, *Gone With The Wind*.

If "no" were to be accepted at face value from the start, most entrepreneurs would end their struggle before they got to first base, in fact, before they even dared to pick up a bat and walk to the plate.

If "no" is not really a final rejection, what *does* it mean? How does an entrepreneur overcome rejection and push a project or idea beyond the obstacles that would block its success?

45

As I mentioned earlier, you will learn a lot about people by how they respond to rejection, to a "no," and even more to an "absolutely, positively, definitely, no!" Here is how dynamos Scott McNealy, Andreas Bechtolsheim, Vinod Khosla, and Bill Joy did not take "no" for an answer and by so doing, started their company and went on to build an empire.

ANDREAS BECHTOLSHEIM, VINOD KHOSLA, BILL JOY,
AND SCOTT McNEALY

ANDREAS BECHTOLSHEIM, VINOD KHOSLA, BILL JOY, AND SCOTT McNEALY OF THE SUN MICROSYSTEMS TEAM

SUN had to get the Computervision contract if the company was to survive. The partners worked feverishly to produce a proposal that they felt was certain to be accepted. Then they were told that Computervision had given the contract to their competitor and wanted to break off all communications with SUN. Khosla and the entire management team drafted what he now calls "the wildest, most aggressive unsolicited proposal ever produced," and within hours were on the red-eye flight to Boston, determined to sleep in Computervision's lobby if necessary. They refused to accept defeat. They had a signed agreement within weeks.

Vinod Khosla, a founder of Daisy Systems Corporation, which manufactures computer-aided engineering workstations, found an article in *Venture Magazine* one day that sent him off to Stanford University and onto a new project that was to prove enormously profitable. The article described the work of Andreas Bechtolsheim, a Stanford Ph.D. candidate in computer science and electrical engineering, who was dissatisfied enough with the computers on the market to build his own. Specifically, the 27-year-old student built his own computer workstation from easily accessible standard components and spare parts. The resulting machine, SUN (named after the Stanford University Network), was low-cost, functional, and efficient, and immediately had Bechtolsheim's friends, professors at the university, and many local companies clamoring for SUNs of their own.

Bechtolsheim had gone with his workstation to several large companies, including Digital Equipment Corporation and IBM, but no one was interested. "Large companies are far behind in terms of their thinking. Typically, they take a long time to introduce new inventions," says Bechtolsheim. "They are very committed to products currently in production. At the time I went to them, they acted as though they would be chopping off the limb they were sitting on if they replaced their one-hundred-thousand-dollar machine with my new ten-thousand-dollar product."

Khosla, however, recognized another start-up opportunity, and convinced Bechtolsheim that a lot of money could be made if they brought the new product to market themselves. Khosla recalls Bechtolsheim's offering him all the technology for about $10,000, to which Khosla replied, "I don't need the golden egg. I want the goose." Bechtolsheim had no idea, however, that less than four years later he and his founding partners would have sold over $350 million worth of his computer.

"The whole thing was really just a case of good luck," says Scott McNealy, whom Khosla brought in to eventually be president and CEO of SUN Microsystems. "Sure, I was planning to own my own company someday, but maybe having a hundred employees when I was fifty and had enough experience is more what I had in mind." McNealy recalls, "Vinod and I were best friends at Stanford Business School. So when he decided to start another company, he called me at ONYX (where McNealy was Director of Operations for the UNIX-based microcomputer manufacturer) and told me that I was going to join them."

Khosla lined up venture capitalists who had backed him in his previous start-up. He prepared a four-page summary business plan that outlined the opportunity. Khosla and McNealy met with Bob Sackman of U.S. Venture Partners and Doug Broyles, a partner in the West Coast Venture Capital Group who previously was the president of ONYX when McNealy started with the company. After a short meeting they left Sackman and Broyles with a handshake and an initial commitment of $50,000 for seed money to start their new venture.

McNealy and Khosla went to McDonald's after the meeting. McNealy remembers, "V.K. [Vinod Khosla] said, 'We have the venture capital, we have the founders, and we have technology. When are you going to quit your job?' I reminded him that he hadn't even given me a job yet." Khosla had something else in mind: "What job? You are a founder!" "So I quit the next day," McNealy says, laughing. "It wasn't as if I had a burning desire to become an entrepreneur. I felt that if it went bad, I still had a Stanford MBA to fall back on, or I could at least get a job pumping gas."

The next day the founders returned to the venture capitalists' office to pick up their $50,000 check. Not wanting to waste any time, they called Bank of America from the venture capitalists' office to open the new account and asked the bank to have the paperwork ready for them to sign. They headed for the bank and within three minutes had run in, made their deposit, and run out with a checkbook. "We spent $10,000 of the $50,000 in our first day in business," said McNealy. They installed new telephones in their temporary office, which was Bechtolsheim's office at Stanford, bought all their office supplies, and made a deposit on their new headquarters, a two-room office with an eight-car garage in Santa Clara.

McNealy, later to be appointed as president, CEO, and chairman of SUN Microsystems, helped guide the growth of SUN from three employees and a two-room office to its present 2,700 employees and one million square feet of facilities in Mountain View, California, with sales offices in 25 countries throughout the world. SUN Microsystems' phenomenal growth—$210 million in sales in its fourth fiscal year—has made it by any standard one of the hottest young companies in the Silicon Valley. But its success was not achieved without meeting many challenges and overcoming many obstacles, including those that might have otherwise been fatal for the company if it were not for the founders' determination.

McNealy remembers, "It was really a wild start. That first $50,000 check seemed like all the money in the world to us. We started calling everyone we knew who could spell UNIX to see who to hire." Bechtolsheim, Khosla, and McNealy all agreed that one of the SUN workstation computer's greatest strengths would be its ability to leverage the AT&T UNIX® operating system. In dozens of phone calls and days of interviews, they would ask, "Who is the best UNIX person in the world?" The name that kept coming up was that of Bill Joy, the brilliant computer scientist at the University of California at Berkeley who pioneered one of the first versions of UNIX and designed and implemented UNIX 4.1BSD for the university. Bechtolsheim agreed with McNealy and Khosla that Joy was the best, but warned: "You'll never get him; Bill makes over $50,000 a year." "Back in those days," says McNealy, "$50,000 a year was a lot of money to us."

The three founders were determined to convince the "UNIX guru" that he should join their team as a fourth founding partner. "V.K. and I called him a number of times and he wouldn't even talk to us. So we all piled into a car and headed up to Berkeley hoping that he would at least talk to Andy Bechtolsheim," says McNealy. Khosla and McNealy, wearing blue jeans, entered Joy's office first. Joy barely acknowledged their presence. "Finally Andy came in and they both went off in Vulcan mind meld talking about UNIX. I knew then we had a perfect marriage of technology and personality," says McNealy.

McNealy later asked Joy why he had ignored him and Khosla when they first came into his office, and Joy sheepishly responded, "I was waiting for top management to walk in." McNealy laughs as he recalls, "We were all 27 at the time. I had had three years of work experience, which was more than the experience of the three other founders combined."

Six weeks later, Joy did agree to join SUN as a founding partner, and the four were off to the races. "With Joy on our team it seemed as if nothing could stop us," says McNealy. They were soon to find out that something almost stopped them permanently.

Early in the development of SUN came a day that McNealy and Khosla still refer to as "Black Monday." SUN had spent almost all its initial venture capital and needed more money to finance continued growth and product development. McNealy and Khosla believed that they had their new financing completely sewed up with the local venture capital firms, Technology Venture Investors (TVI) and Kleiner, Perkins, Caufield, and Byers. When they walked into TVI's office on Monday to pick up their check, Dave Marquardt of TVI told them that although TVI had previously indicated they would provide SUN with the money, they had changed their minds and decided not to invest. The partners immediately visited John Doerr at Kleiner, Perkins, Caufield, and Byers, only to find out that his firm had decided to wait for TVI's investment.

According to McNealy, TVI's and Kleiner Perkins's change of heart was due to their discovery that McNealy and Khosla had started a company weeks before they started SUN. The company, Data Dump, was a losing investment for all involved. TVI and Kleiner Perkins were displeased with McNealy and Khosla for not telling them about their previous failure.

"We walked out of the meeting totally shocked. It could have meant we would have to close the door," says McNealy. "But we wouldn't take no for an answer. Three months of hard selling later, we closed the deal with TVI and Kleiner Perkins at a higher price." SUN subsequently also obtained $20 million in venture capital investment from Eastman Kodak.

One rule that McNealy says he learned from the experience is always to raise money before you need it, not when you need it. Other important rules he follows are never go into an important negotiation alone, and always make friends because every enemy you have will sooner or later reappear to make you miserable. But perhaps the most important tenet of McNealy's business philosophy and SUN's corporate culture is "work as hard today as during the first few days of the start-up." "You must have a maniacal sense of urgency," says McNealy. "You must be totally efficient, yet at the speed of light. There is no magic to being successful. You just have to work harder and faster than the competition."

McNealy says one of his main jobs is to keep the corporate culture current and crisp by reminding SUN's 2700 employees, more than half of whom have joined in the past 12 months, about how hard they need to work to ensure the company's success as it grows.

"If rule number one is to work hard," says McNealy, "rule number zero is never give up and never take no for an answer." McNealy believes that anything really important usually takes at least a few rejections or failures before success is achieved. "Only after people say no to me at least a dozen times will I begin to take them seriously. Only then will I start to consider an alternative way to approach them."

That philosophy literally saved SUN's life in mid-1983. Its main competitor, Apollo Computers, had all but shut out SUN from a major position in the workstation marketplace. Apollo was in the market years ahead of SUN and had contracts with Mentor, Calma, and Autotrol. In the foreseeable future, only one major CAD (computer-aided design) vendor was going to sign up with a workstation manufacturer. That was Computervision, which was the largest CAD supplier in the world. "We moved into a big new building to try to impress them," says McNealy, "but it was an uphill battle; Apollo was the big rising star going public, and we were the struggling little guy." McNealy was convinced that SUN had to get the Computervision contract to survive in the industry. Without at least one major visible customer in the marketplace, people would say that SUN had no future.

The partners worked feverishly on producing what they believed was a proposal certain to be accepted. Then came the decision, in a fateful phone call on a Thursday afternoon. "V.K. answered the phone and I saw him go white, which for V.K. (whose family is from India) is very hard to do. I knew something terrible had happened," says McNealy. The phone call was from Computervision's purchasing department. The caller told them that they had given the contract to Apollo and wanted to break off all communications with SUN. "That was the first day, after Black Monday, when closing the door seemed like it could be a reality," says McNealy. "Apollo would have become the undisputed standard in the industry, and we could never hope to compete."

Khosla immediately pulled the entire management team together and drafted what he refers to as the "wildest, most aggressive unsolicited proposal ever produced." Within hours they had raced it to the Federal Express office, and Khosla and other top officers were boarding the red-eye flight to Boston, determined to sleep in Computervision's lobby if necessary.

Khosla and his team of managers and technicians waited in Computervision's lobby for hours the next morning. No one would even come down to see them. Finally, one friend who worked at Computervision came down and said that corporate policy strictly stated that no one from Computervision was to talk with SUN. But after some encouragement from Khosla and associates, he agreed to talk senior management into setting up a meeting.

A couple of weeks and numerous phone calls and Federal Express packages later, SUN had a secret negotiation session with the top management of Computervision at O'Hare International Airport in Chicago. Part of the sweetener offered in the negotiations was SUN's agreement to offer equity incentives approximating 2.5 percent of SUN's then outstanding stock in exchange for a $40 million Computervision contract. Within weeks after their meeting SUN had a signed agreement with Computervision. According to McNealy, if SUN had not won that contract it wouldn't be where it is today, and might not even be in business. "Our goal today is to treat every contract like the Computervision contract, like a matter of life and death. No company ever went out of business for doing too much business," says McNealy.

A lot of companies talk about being market-driven, but most SUN officers focus on being customer-driven, with an emphasis on *driven*. "The customer knows what he wants; what you have to do is listen," emphasizes McNealy. SUN manufactures its workstations using an open-system approach, which provides customers the flexibility to use the SUN equipment in conjunction with other computer manufacturers' peripherals and equipment. SUN uses standard components that allow customers to tie into existing systems without making them obsolete. SUN also provides a UNIX-based system, something that is highly desirable among its users, who are primarily in the engineering and science fields. Apollo, its major competitor, pushes proprietary technologies.

Many customers praise SUN for producing a very high-quality and high-resolution workstation. Comments McNealy, "What is proprietary to us is the art of making a Ferrari out of spare parts." Among SUN's growing list of customers are AT&T, Toshiba, Gould, Schlumberger, General Motors, Teradyne, and the University of California at Berkeley. SUN divides its sales 50 percent to the OEM (original equipment manufacturer) market and 50 percent to end users. SUN's workstation prices range from $8,000 to $70,000.

Another important part of the SUN business philosophy is its focus on "real value." Says Khosla, "Our philosophy is, let's do stuff of real value for whomever we do it—real value will always come through in the end." SUN did not spend a single penny on advertising for more than three years. "If we advertise, our customers will not really get anything out of it," says Khosla. "Every time we had an advertising budget it would get canceled at the last minute. The five hundred thousand dollars in an ad budget could be put to better use for us and provide greater value to our customers if we used it to hire ten more engineers for our customer support staff." SUN believes if you put your money into developing the best product, your sales in the long run will go further than if you put the same amount of money into advertising.

With the recent funding from its public stock offering and movement into other markets for its workstations, SUN has set aside a small advertising budget for this year. "Unfortunately, the world isn't ideal," says Khosla. "A high-level manager of a big company, who makes ten-million-dollar purchase decisions, often won't purchase the product unless he is familiar with the company name and has seen it in the trade journals. That doesn't justify using advertising to push a product, but for familiarity, it's okay. You have to remember that it is the product that's selling."

The advent of SUN's first advertising expenditures doesn't mean the company is growing soft, by any means. "We still make our money go two to three times as far as our competitors and our revenue per employee is much higher than the competition's," says Khosla. When SUN moved into its new headquarters the furniture was kept simple, functional, and inexpensive. "One day someone put up a piece of art in the front lobby that cost hundreds of dollars, and within fifteen minutes Scott took it off the wall and had it returned," says Khosla. "It pays to be very careful with your own expenses so you can afford to put quality into the product."

One of the greatest problems faced by any young company is how to manage growth effectively. SUN's fast growth rate has been nothing short of phenomenal. Sales grew from $86,000 in fiscal 1982, $8.7 million in fiscal 1983, $39 million in fiscal 1984, and $115 million in fiscal 1985 to $210 million in fiscal 1986. McNealy claims SUN has been able to manage its rapid growth through its policy of hiring over-qualified people in every position, particularly management. Although at 31 the founders are all still very young, the average age of SUN management is over 40. "We have the best of both worlds," said Khosla, "a healthy mix of inexperienced people who didn't know what couldn't be done and experienced people—freaky scientists and pragmatic managers, bright upstarts and seasoned veterans."

"We want to be a billion-dollar-plus company," says McNealy. "You can't afford to hire people who don't have the vision for growth. You need to hire overqualified people so you won't cap your growth—as the company grows their jobs will grow into their full capacity." McNealy cites Darryl Barbé as an example of SUN hiring strategy. Barbé, who previously ran a $500 million division of Digital Equipment Corporation (DEC) and managed 2500 people, was selected as the first SUN Employee for Europe. Obviously Barbé was overqualified for the position, and it was quite a change at first for him to work without a staff of 2500, but SUN maintains that if they want to build their European operations to several hundred million dollars plus in business then they have the right person for the job. SUN has attracted many other top managers and engineers from companies such as Hewlett-Packard, Xerox, Amdahl, Apollo, and Apple.

McNealy often uses his father's hiring strategy as a guide. His father, previously vice chairman of American Motors and president of AMF, believed in hiring managers who are athletic and whose academic records are above average but not necessarily excellent. The former supplies endurance and the latter ensures a more well-rounded individual who can get along with people. McNealy uses this guide for hiring managers, but for engineers he prefers employees with top academic records and strong discipline.

McNealy also stresses that SUN has hired a lot of top talent due to his "strategic alliances" with his former friends at the Stanford Business School. "It pays to make friends and build alliances in school as well as industry," says McNealy. "Developing a good relationship with classmates allows you to cut through all the B.S. when you are doing business with them later. For example, if it wasn't for my friendship with V.K., I might still be at ONYX."

Another management principle that SUN employs is to provide people with responsibility and the authority to make decisions within their fields, so they can work unhampered by overlapping responsibilities from other departments. "We left technology to the technologists and management to the managers," says McNealy. Cofounder Bill Joy agrees that his unwillingness to get involved in direct management has helped SUN steer clear of problems that have faced many of the industry's technical pioneers when they became entrepreneurs.

McNealy stresses that being an entrepreneur is mentally demanding and physically grueling. "People who get involved in a start-up have to make significant trade-offs between business and personal time. Your friends have to be very understanding, and you'd better have been very happily married for a long time, or else single, because if you are in the middle ground, you soon *will* be single." (McNealy, Bechtolsheim, and Joy are single.) Recently, the company made a $45 million public offering, which was managed by underwriters Robertson, Colman, and Stephens and Alex Brown and Sons. To promote the offering, McNealy went on a two-week road show that included stops in San Francisco, Los Angeles, Dallas, Minneapolis, New York, Boston, Hartford, Baltimore, London, Edinburgh, and Paris. He saw as many as seven different audiences a day.

Bechtolsheim agrees with McNealy. "It pays to start when you are young; once you have house payments and family responsibilities it's fairly hard. Also, you don't have the same energy level when you are over thirty." Bechtolsheim recalls the time when he had to invest his life savings in the company. "I only had me to worry about, and I didn't mind taking the risk, so I felt, what the heck? and I did it."

All the founders' investments have surely paid off. Their individual stock holdings have a current value of $10 to $20 million each. Khosla has achieved his goal of retiring before the age of 30 and devotes his time to "numerous leisure activities." But he does admit to being a part-time partner with Kleiner, Perkins, Caufield, and Byers. "Part time," says Khosla, "because I don't want to work full time anymore." Anyone who knows Khosla will tell you that he will soon be out of retirement, off and running with his next project.

Bechtolsheim, Joy, and McNealy are still at the helm of the SUN management team, and in spite of their recently acquired wealth, they are not about to rest on their laurels. With IBM and DEC looming overhead with their recent entries into the workstation market, industry analysts claim that SUN is going to be facing even tougher competition in the future. But that doesn't worry SUN very much. Comments McNealy, "We are still hungry and looking for lunch."

"I WOULD RATHER PLAY THE GAME THAN WRITE THE RULES"— PROFESSIONALS TURNED ENTREPRENEURS

Avy Stein, chairman of Regent Corporation, typifies the recent move of motivated young people out of the legal profession and into entrepreneurship. For years, lawyers often stood on the sidelines and watched their clients reap riches in the deals they put together, while the law firm's up side was limited to its $150 per hour billing rate.

The *New York Times* and the *Wall Street Journal* have recently chronicled the exodus of young lawyers from the top law firms into the ranks of investment banking. Seeing that there is more money to be made, as well as fun to be had, by putting together profitable deals as opposed to doing the research and writing the contracts, lawyers have begun to make their march on Wall Street. As Avy Stein so eloquently put it, "I would rather play the game than write the rules." For other young attorneys and professionals considering similar pursuits, the story to follow will show how one of their colleagues made the transformation.

AVY STEIN

AVY STEIN OF REGENT CORPORATION

"There is only one thing certain about inflation, interest rates, and oil prices—they are going to change." Avy Stein says he looks for two kinds of deals, undervalued or down markets or fragmented industries which other people shy away from. "Besides," says Stein, "people never made money by coming in on the top of the market."

Avy Stein didn't just want to start a business, he wanted to create a conglomerate. And he did. Stein, 31, is the founder, principal owner, and shareholder of Regent Corporation, which owns Regent Energy, an oil and gas exploration and acquisition partnership sponsor; Regent Properties, a real estate management and holding company; Regent Benefits, an insurance company; and Regent Equities, which provides products to pension funds, corporations, and individual investors. Stein's background is not entrepreneurial. His story is more that of a highly paid corporate lawyer who, after years of practicing corporate law, learned that there is more money to be made in playing the game than in writing the rules.

Stein grew up in Chicago. At 13 he was sent to the Peddie Prep School, mainly because, according to Stein, "My father felt that he couldn't control my wildness." Stein was soon to return to Chicago—"I got upset because there were no girls around"—and he later attended the University of Illinois as an accounting major. Stein's sport in college was ice hockey; however, an accident that necessitated the removal of two discs and a piece of his spine forced him to give up the sport. The five-foot-five Stein likes to joke, "Before the accident I used to be six-foot-four."

Stein admits that throughout most of high school and college he really didn't know what he wanted to do. He took the CPA exam in his senior year of college and passed all parts of it. He also took the Law School Admissions Test (LSAT) and did well enough to gain admission to Harvard Law School. Says Stein, "I did not know what I wanted to do but I figured if I could get into Harvard I probably should go."

After graduation, Stein joined the Chicago-based law firm of Kirkland & Ellis. In his first year Stein achieved great success by what he calls "getting lucky," but which another observer might attribute to Stein's own efforts. He was asked to work on *National Business List vs. Dun & Bradstreet*, a case that was a combination of antitrust and copyright litigation. One night a junior partner asked him to complete a cross-examination for the case. Stein finished the assignment at 2 A.M. the next morning, but he wasn't happy with the way the cross-examination was originally outlined. During the next four hours he wrote his own cross-examination, and offered both the original and his version to Fred Bartlit, the nationally renowned senior partner and trial lawyer of Stein's firm. Stein says he had never seen anyone as masterful in court as Bartlit, and he wanted to impress him so he could work with him in the future. Bartlit was impressed with the cross-examination Stein had created and with his personal initiative. Bartlit commented that it took guts to do this, and he asked Stein to prepare his other cross-examination outlines in the case. For the next two years Stein was a trial lawyer working directly with Bartlit and other senior partners.

Stein soon decided he wanted to take advantage of his CPA background and work on business deals. When the opportunity arose to move to the firm's new Denver office he seized it. He expected it would be a situation in which he could do both business and litigation. Stein felt he could learn deal-negotiating skills from the firm's top corporate strategist, J. Landis (Lanny) Martin, who was the office's managing partner. "Lanny is a true leader," says Stein. In Denver, Stein worked on real estate and oil and gas transactions. He also was asked to negotiate a new office lease for Kirkland & Ellis when they needed to move to new and larger offices. In 1982, Kirkland & Ellis moved to 1999 Broadway in Denver on a lease negotiated by Stein and Lanny Martin that was such a bargain for the firm that the story was the subject of an article in *Fortune Magazine*. The *Fortune* article claimed the law firm received over $2.2 million up front from the office building developers to move their offices into the building. Stein says that the firm actually received more cash and that the agreement netted a lease cost of less than three dollars per square foot for a 10-year period. Stein said of his achievement, "That really made me think that maybe I would be better off negotiating for my own account."

But Stein was to gain more deal-making experience before venturing off on his own. He developed a strong relationship with the Madsen Company to work on their property development deals. Through work he was doing for Hamilton Oil Corporation, Stein brought in a new client, Cook International, and he learned the oil and gas business as rapidly as he had learned about real estate. Cook was then being traded on the American Stock Exchange, and Ned Cook, the flamboyant founder and chairman, soon became friends with Stein. Stein helped Cook work out a couple of troublesome oil and gas deals and Cook remarked, "You are one of the only lawyers that I work with who has the business sense to know what I should do and the guts to tell me." Stein enjoyed working with Cook, and soon he was billing his hours to Cook on a steady basis. Stein noticed that his lawyer's salary was only a small fraction of the money the deals produced for the entrepreneurs Madsen and Cook. Again Stein realized that he would be better off negotiating for his own account.

Cook and Stein were soon to work out a deal in which Stein would join Cook as president of the energy subsidiary and as vice president in charge of corporate planning and legal affairs for the parent, Cook International. At the time Cook Energy had $25 million worth of assets and $12 million in debt, but due to a few bad oil and gas projects the company was losing money. Cook originally was a grain trading company—the first company to trade grain with the Soviet Union. Cook later plunged into the oil and gas development and insurance business and acquired Terminix, the nation's second largest pest control company. Says Stein, "Cook's energy operations were losing money, the insurance business was just about breaking even or worse and Terminix was going like gangbusters." Stein and the company's other executives carried out a strategy to liquidate the oil and gas assets, to maintain the pest control business, and to use the proceeds from the oil and gas liquidation to take the company private. They were able to generate $14 million after paying off all debts and quickly purchased all outstanding shares of the parent company not in the company's control group.

Stein started looking for oil and gas acquisition targets. He wanted the firm to move its resources into more profitable oil and gas and investment ventures, but his plan was soon interrupted by the IRS and a drastic change in Terminix's insurance rates. "The IRS began to make ridiculously loud noises regarding an old group of grain trades made in the early and mid-1970s and demanded large payments. Meanwhile, our insurance rates at Terminix more than doubled. The banks became more difficult to work with. I had put together what appeared to be great oil and gas deals, but Ned Cook kept holding me back and telling me 'no' because money was tight." As Stein continued to work out Cook's problems and raise money for the company, he again realized that his work was benefiting others more than himself. He decided to make his move. Stein made a proposal to acquire assets from Cook Energy. The deal was struck in September 1985 and closed in November of that year.

Stein was able to take over the company in a leveraged transaction in which he combined investment capital, bank loans, and some shrewd sales of assets in order to begin his new operation. Stein restructured the company and founded Regent Corporation, which is focused on direct venture investments, real estate and oil and gas syndications, insurance products and other investment opportunities.

Within the first month after the acquisition, Stein closed his new company's first real estate deal. He and his employees raised $1.6 million to acquire a shopping center in Southwest Denver. Soon afterward he opened the company's new insurance division and hired one of the best salespeople in the area, providing him with incentives, including stock in the new company.

To expand his capital-raising abilities, Stein then hired John Walsh, a seventeen-year veteran and ex-partner of Touche, Ross & Co. and a former Regional Vice President of Integrated Resources, Inc., to run the equity placement subsidiary.

Stein maintains that his first-year game plan has changed substantially. Initially, Regent Energy Corporation planned to drill 12 wells in 1986; Regent Properties, Inc., which already had acquired a $7.45 million shopping center, planned to acquire approximately $15 million in additional real estate assets before the end of the year; and venture capital/leveraged buyout transactions would begin toward year end. But venture capital and leveraged buyout transactions have moved to the forefront.

Flexibility thus far has been the key for Stein. Plunging oil prices and tax reform made it difficult to sell oil and gas and real estate programs. Regent, therefore, altered its course to emphasize high current yield venture capital transactions. Regent has raised approximately $30 million on its way to a business plan calling for well in excess of $100 million of equity to buy and become partners with companies in the security alarm business. Stein has placed several million dollars in this industry at extremely high cash-on-cash returns for his investors. He also has purchased control of Security Alliance Corporation, one of the largest independent franchise organizations in the security alarm business, which gave him security alarm dealerships in 30 states.

A combination of factors set Regent's course. Stein and his equity placement specialist, John Walsh, determined that to expand rapidly their equity placement activities, they needed an untainted product (not real estate or oil and gas) and an innovative product (not cable TV) that would present high immediate cash yields plus appreciation potential. "Investors are tired of waiting for appreciation and lights at the end of the tunnel. They still like a sexy upside, but immediate cash yield is critical. Obviously, tax benefits are less impressive as well." With those parameters in mind, Stein went back to his earlier experiences with Terminix pest control and other recurring revenue businesses. Stein decided to raise in excess of $100 million to acquire companies and assets in the fragmented security alarm business. "Security alarm monitoring recurring revenues were underpriced as compared to cable TV, pest control, and pay telephones. The industry also was extremely fragmented and undercapitalized. Approximately $1.5 billion in recurring revenues was controlled by 11,000 independent companies. Changing pricing philosophies by, and competition from, big players were placing an extraordinary need for capital on these companies. Therefore, we believed we could be the main force in consolidating this fragmented industry while at the same time yielding investors returns averaging 20 to 30 percent per year. The security alarm business allowed us to develop our high current yield investment product with sexy upside potential."

Through its various enterprises, Regent has affiliates in thirty states and is growing rapidly. Says Stein, "We hope to be seen as the preeminent provider of specialty investment products to institutions, corporations, and individuals. At the same time, we will be expanding our product lines so that our marketing and sales force will grow faster."

According to Stein, Regent is unique in that it always invests its own money alongside its investors' money. "We are trying to be a Merchant Bank which provides products and services," says Stein. Stein also structures deals with extremely strong performance incentives. Even Regent's partnership management fee in deals is subordinate to an above market return to Stein's investors. "I have to perform to make money on deals; why not?" says Stein.

Stein looks to build his company by continuing to hire quality people. He points to the fact that Regent uses lawyers and accountants both as due diligence officers and as salespeople because they understand the investments and are able to define properly the benefits to the customer. Stein hopes to maintain Regent's "selling style" by sticking to trained professionals instead of just hiring superhot salespeople, but recognizes the need for strong sales talent.

Stein projects first-year cash revenues for all of his entities will be approximately $5 million, with a net profit of $750,000. This figure does not include the value of the firm's equity share in the investment projects, which is typically 20 to 40 percent of each deal after the investors earn their above market preferred return from the transaction. Five years down the road Stein hopes to do in excess of $300 million in annual equity placements. Currently, Regent and its direct affiliates (companies that Stein controls) have approximately 40 employees who work directly for the Corporation and nearly an additional 1000 people involved in various aspects of business transacted by Regent entities. Three of Regent's key executives collectively own 12 percent of the Corporation: the balance is owned by Stein and private investors, with Stein owning in excess of 75 percent of Regent. Stein has granted and intends to continue to grant Regent stock options to key personnel.

Regarding his investment philosophy, Stein says, "We look for undervalued situations in businesses we can understand thoroughly, especially in fragmented, undercapitalized industries. There is only one thing certain about inflation, interest rates, oil prices, and venture opportunities—they are going to change. You have to be versatile and thoroughly know the industries you are in to sustain an investment business over time." "Besides," says Stein, "people never made money by coming in on the top of the market."

"ONE DAY I JUST WOKE UP WITH A GREAT IDEA"

As mentioned earlier, a typical dynamo is one who after thinking of a new idea in the shower, jumps out and starts putting it to work. Unfortunately, most people simply just dry off and forget their idea during the course of a day. The following chapters represent examples of idea men and women who put their ideas into action.

Sometimes, for true entrepreneurs, an inferior product or a long wait in line at a local shop is the spark that fires a new enterprise rather than an inconvenience or a disappointment. Steve Kirsch grumbled about the poor performance of a mechanical computer control device, called a "mouse," that he was using—and decided a better one needed to be developed. Kirsch subsequently did just that, and his company, Mouse Systems, grew to over $10 million in sales.

Whereas some entrepreneurs find opportunity in the poor performance of existing products, others see opportunities in providing new products to feed the changing tastes and habits of our fast-paced, constantly evolving society. Sophia Collier and Connie Best had the foresight years ago to see that, with growing health food consciousness in the late 1970s,

73

these concerns would spill over not only into the food we eat but also the sodas we drink. They were the developers of the first natural sodas. Their vision led to a major innovation in the soft drink market; even the major bottlers are now following suit with similar products. Julie Brice also saw the trend among Americans for low-fat, healthier food. She bet on yogurt vs. ice cream; now she has a fast-growing franchise network throughout the United States.

In today's get-ahead oriented society, young professionals have developed an almost unquenchable thirst for career advancement knowledge. Books like *Dress for Success* have become bestsellers. The seminar company founded by young dynamos Jimmy Calano and Jeff Salzman became a major contender in the training industry by offering seminars that people wanted and at a price they could afford.

How do you find a good business idea? The answer still lies in the simple quotation from Andrew Carnegie: "Find a need and fill it." But remember, just finding the idea is not enough. If it were that easy, everyone would be rich. You will only profit if you work toward implementing your idea so that it develops as a business opportunity.

STEVE KIRSCH

STEVE KIRSCH OF MOUSE SYSTEMS CORPORATION

"Here you had three $100,000 machines that were crippled because the mechanical mice were broken. It was like having a Ferrari with only three wheels on it. I thought there had to be a better way."

"**B**uild a better mousetrap and the world will beat a path to your door." Steve Kirsch went one step further: He built a better mouse. His "mouse" is a little square box with button controls. Used alongside a computer keyboard, it speeds the flow of data, graphics, and word processing across the instrument's screen.

It all started when Kirsch was a student at MIT. "I was sitting in a room with three very expensive computers. All of them were using mechanical mice and all the mice were dead. I thought it was pretty sad—here you had three $100,000 machines that were crippled because the mechanical mice were broken. It was like having a Ferrari with only three wheels on it. I thought there had to be a better way." Kirsch devised a better way and proceeded to develop it. The result was an optical, rather than mechanical, mouse. There are no moving parts in Kirsch's mouse, so, unlike mechanical mice, it lasts long and is free of breakage and maintenance problems. It works by counting the number of lines it moves across on a two-color grid aluminum mouse pad.

Kirsch started out on his own in July 1982 and six months later built his first 300 mice in the living room of his Sunnyvale, California apartment. They sold out as fast as he could produce them. Six months after that, he raised $300,000 in initial financing through Whitney Ventures of Mountain View, and within six months, sales hit $2 million. To fund their growth the company later raised an additional $2 million in venture capital from Walden Management, Assets Management Co. and Summerhill Partners and arranged a $1 million line of credit at Silicon Valley Bank. The company currently has over 70 employees and produced over $10 million in sales for 1985.

Kirsch, now 29, looks back on the company's early beginnings and phenomenal growth with a smile and a bit of humor. "When I first got started at my apartment there was a woman vendor who refused to come see us. She said she was afraid to, especially since we were then calling the company Rodent Associates." Vickie Blakeslee, employee number three and current manager of administration, had a hard time letting her former associates at University of California at Berkeley know that she was working out of some guy's living room. Explains Kirsch, "I didn't have a garage so I had to use my living room." As for the initial name of his company, "Well, we were doing a demo at Convergent Technologies, and one of the engineers asked what the name of the company was. I said I didn't know yet, and he said, 'Why don't you call it Rodent Associates?' "

Before Kirsch set up shop in his apartment, he worked on licensing his first prototype, a mouse running on a checkerboard style grid to determine direction. He spent a year before finding a company, Summagraphics Corp., that would agree to license his technology. In the meantime, Kirsch left MIT in 1981 to work for ROLM Corporation in California. While working for ROLM, he developed Mouse System's current method of building their mice. Kirsch quit his job at ROLM. "I didn't feel I could change the world there as fast as I wanted to."

Kirsch believed that Summagraphics was failing to market his technology and was dragging its feet; he decided to develop & market the mouse on his own. But Summagraphics refused to release the license to him. Faced with this dilemma, Kirsch decided to spend "three months skiing and three months watching TV." Says Kirsch, "I tried to look for a job but nobody would hire me. I was unemployable. I tried to look for a job in which I could have an impact. I looked for ads that said 'Here you can change the world.' " But no such ad existed and Kirsch decided that his only option was to go out on his own and develop and market the mouse, knowing that by doing it, he risked being sued by Summagraphics.

Kirsch later brought the product to market and sold 300 units. Subsequently, Summagraphics brought a suit against him, but it was settled by giving Summagraphics and Mouse Systems joint use of the patents under license. Summagraphics, along with Microsoft and Logitech, which make nonoptical mice, is now a Mouse Systems' competitor. Mouse Systems is currently the largest independent domestic-based producer of mice.

Says Kirsch, "We introduced our mouse about the same time Apple introduced the Macintosh, which also uses a mouse. It helped us gain credibility. What we did in order to sell our mice through retail computer stores was to create some pop-up menu software that could be used with any existing software. It works quite well with Lotus 1-2-3, for example."

"Pop-up menus" are windows that appear on the computer screen when the user wants to use a new command or review the software program's instructions. The pop-up menus eliminate the need to memorize many different complex commands. They also allow the user to select a function simply by moving the mouse until the arrow on the screen points to the function desired, useful for such operations as removing a word in a word processor without using a keyboard or edit without memorizing computer program commands. By providing his mice with software that made it easy to use with the best-selling software programs, Kirsch received ready acceptance for his mice.

The use of mice is becoming widespread. The market for mice as projected by Dataquest will grow from 307,000 units in 1984 to 9.1 million units in 1989.

Mouse Systems' initial big break came from SUN Microsystems (SUN is covered in another chapter) which provided them with $11,000 in funding to develop a mouse for their new computer workstation. "In fact Andy (one of the three founders of SUN) was a big help to me," says Kirsch. "He helped me design the mouse, and I developed the tracking algorithm on a SUN workstation." Mouse currently produces all the mice used for the SUN Microsystems workstations. SUN along with Computervision, Concept Technology, Masscomp, Silicon Graphics, and Texas Instruments, is a major OEM customer. As Mouse Systems outgrew Kirsch's apartment they moved into SUN's old headquarters at Commerce Campus. Mouse Systems later moved across the street to their present 23,000-square-foot facility in Santa Clara.

Kirsch said that he tried raising money during the early stages of the company's development but was unsuccessful. "There were three reasons. I had no business experience; we were trying to create a market that was as yet unproven; we did not have a management team. In January of 1984, Bob Dickinson joined the company as president at the recommendation of the venture capital investors. Dickinson manages the corporate growth while Kirsch remains chairman and vice president of research and development. Dickinson, 44, came to Mouse from Zilog's Computer Systems division where as general manager he doubled the division's sales within one year. Dickinson worked on raising more capital for Mouse Systems and brought in more management, drawing talent from Wang Labs, Hewlett-Packard, Apple, Western Digital, Memorex, Zilog, and Singer to staff his management team.

While Dickinson runs an efficient corporate agenda, Kirsch maintains a creative entrepreneurial atmosphere among the staff. Probably the best way to compare Dickinson's and Kirsch's management styles can be seen by comparing the way they conduct corporate meetings. While Dickinson's presentations are filled with graphs and charts representing productivity, sales growth, and market share, Kirsch conducts meetings that feature commercials, gossip columns, and entertainment, including one show entitled "This is Your Life, Bob Dickinson." At Kirsch's show for Dickinson he presented him with "the First Annual Kirsch Pie Award" with instructions that Bob could throw the whipped cream pie at the Mouse officer of his choosing. "Of course, I came prepared," said Kirsch, who donned a raincoat just before offering the pie to Dickinson.

While Kirsch credits Dickinson for his strong management and leadership abilities, Kirsch takes it upon himself to ensure that work is fun, and he finds many creative ways to do that. Another example of Kirsch's rather unique sense of humor was his decision about what he should wear at a television show in which top corporate management were to speak. Everyone wondered if Steve was going to appear in his usual attire of blue jeans and sneakers—maybe put on a tie for the occasion. "Our VP of Engineering told me that he was going to dress up so I thought I would too." Kirsch showed up the next day dressed up like a woman. "Of course I did change just before the show," says Kirsch, "but not everyone was sure that I would." A number of company engineers later confirmed that's just par for the course for Steve.

Kirsch sees a future where computers will become much more advanced and will be found in more aspects of our everyday life. "The ultimate machine will be able to negotiate the price of a new car for you." Mouse Systems currently is selling software programs in addition to their mice. Their "PC Paint" program provides versatile color graphics for the IBM Personal Computer and has been rated one of its top 10 software programs. Down the road, Kirsch sees Mouse Systems offering more business graphics products and continuing its expansion into foreign markets. Mouse Systems has entered into a joint venture with SMK Corporation to market its products in Japan.

Kirsch explains his plan for his own future in two parts: first, to have fun and second, to do something significant. He points to the more than 100,000 people who use his mice every day and says, "We have succeeded in making a difference in their lives. What we want to do in the future is continue to make people's work environment more productive."

Not unlike Steve Jobs, who resigned from Apple and established Next, Steve Kirsch on April 1, 1986 resigned from Mouse Systems to start another company, Frame Technology. According to Kirsch, "The date was significant: I felt like a fool for resigning, but I've been interested in hypertext technology for the last six years. In fact, it was only after failing to find a job in that area that I started Mouse. But now I think I can make it work." Kirsch's new company will start off by creating desktop publishing software for the SUN workstation. He claims that his new company will actually expand the sales of Mouse Systems by creating new applications for the use of the Mouse.

CONNIE BEST AND SOPHIA COLLIER

SOPHIA COLLIER AND CONNIE BEST OF AMERICAN NATURAL BEVERAGE CORP.

They intend to compete by investing in the good quality of their product. From a small business standpoint, the founders believe it is safer to make a better product than to focus on promotion. Promotion takes revenues out of the product, quality puts it in.

Sophia Collier has been a leader and a person of intense individualism. Her autobiography *Soul Rush: The Odyssey of a Young Woman of the Seventies* (William Morrow & Co., 1977), tells how, after graduating from high school at 16, she lived on a Hopi Indian reservation, built sailboats on western Mexico's Sea of Cortez, and managed a New England food cooperative. Collier later started a construction business, Portland American Contracting, in Maine by hiring a retired contractor to help her estimate jobs while she posed as her own secretary. "No one awarding construction bids would have taken a teenaged woman contractor seriously," she says.

At 29, Sophia Collier is president of American Natural Beverage Corp., which makes all-natural carbonated beverages. The company's sales last year exceeded $10 million, the current sales rate for 1986 is in excess of $20 million. Collier's all-natural sodas, Soho Natural Soda, were the first in the United States to introduce real fruit juice into their soda products. The recipe for Soho Natural Soda was first formulated by Collier in 1978, working out of her Brooklyn, New York apartment. She was looking to develop a fresh tasting soda using no preservatives or artificial ingredients. Her taste had long outgrown the sugary sodas that inundated the marketplace. She was betting that if people were presented with a healthier, better tasting alternative that contained real fruit juice instead of sugar and artificial flavors, they would buy it. With the $10,000 in royalties she had received from her book, an additional $10,000 from an investor, and the aid of her business partner and cofounder, Connie Best, Soho Natural Soda was introduced in the fall of 1978.

Collier's bet paid off; she sold more than 72,000 bottles by year's end. Sales continued to skyrocket, going to two million bottles in 1983, four million bottles in 1984, and eight million bottles in 1985.

Soho Natural Soda's success is based on the entrepreneurial spirit of the founders and the growing market of health-conscious Americans. American Natural Beverage Corp. literally created an entire new market in the soft drink industry. "Most people older and wiser would have never done it," says 32-year-old Best. "The beverage industry contains two of the largest marketing organizations in the world, Coke and Pepsi, and you don't mess with Coke and Pepsi." Collier and Best say that although they are not yet the same size or as well known as Canada Dry, they intend to be within the next few years.

Since Soho Natural pioneered the market, about a dozen natural brands have jumped in to compete for a piece of the soda market. Even Coca-Cola and Pepsi have sat up and taken notice; they have already started test marketing carbonated fruit juice drinks. But Collier and Best say they are not worried, because although they do not have anywhere near the money to compete with Coke's or Pepsi's advertising campaigns, they intend to compete by investing in the good quality of their product. Says Best, "Good quality means tasting very good. Advertising can get your product on the shelf but the only real reason people will reorder and regularly buy your soda is because they like how it tastes, not because of advertising, image, and all the other phoney baloney." From a small business standpoint, the founders believe it is safer to make a better product than to focus on promotion. Promotion takes revenues out of the product, quality puts it in. Says Best, "You don't want to advertise to empty shelves."

Collier and Best, both vegetarian and health food purists, continue to emphasize natural fruit flavor and taste in their products. Soho's all natural flavors include Ginseng Ginger-Ale, Black Cherry, Orange, Lemon-Lime, Fruit Punch, Grape, Raspberry, Root Beer, Cream, Lemon Spritzer (no calories), and Sparkling Water (no sodium). All the water for the sodas is drawn from deep wells and triple filtered. Soho Natural Soda is distributed in individual 12-ounce bottles and four-packs of 12-ounce bottles and cans with an award-winning label and packaging designed by Doug Johnson. The label is very bright and classy and in the style of what might be designed as an advertising poster for the Beatle movie *The Yellow Submarine*. Collier says, "We wanted our packaging to represent the unique, fresh taste found inside the bottle."

Among Soho Natural's customers are Bloomingdale's and Macy's; the Helmsley Palace Hotel in New York, the Hyatt Regency in San Francisco, and the Marriott Corporation; the 7-11, Kroger, Sloan, D'Agostino, and Safeway stores. Today Soho Natural Sodas are selling to health and premium food outlets, primarily in urban markets, through a nationwide network of distributors. Soho Natural is sold in over 1500 stores in the New York metropolitan area alone. The company has also negotiated agreements for the Japanese and Saudi Arabian markets and has opened West Coast offices in San Francisco. Currently, all the bottling is done in two independent bottling facilities in Pennsylvania and California. The partners also plan to set up other bottling arrangements throughout the United States.

Best realizes that they will need more investment capital as they grow. "We were initially capitalized at $20,000, which was painfully inadequate—as we were soon to learn," says Best. The two founders have shown that they have the ability to manage growth; they are not interested in taking on professional venture capital partners who might want them to step aside and to replace them and their staff with former executives of Coca-Cola. "That would destroy our product as well as the atmosphere here," says Best. "Our people are committed to our company, they have clarity and enthusiasm. We like running the company and so do the people who work here—we intend to keep it that way."

During 1983, Collier formulated a fountain syrup version of the Soho Natural Soda flavors to be distributed nationally through Haagen-Dazs ice cream shops and other premium food stores. This program is expanding as American Natural Beverage Corp. places its own Soho Natural Soda fountain systems in the restaurants, department stores, snack franchises, and movie theaters along the East Coast. "I noticed that the biggest bottlers have a stranglehold on the syrup used by soda fountains and fast food stores," says Collier. "So now that we are making Soho Natural syrup we will be available everywhere and become an enduring part of the American landscape. We're shooting for sales of $100 million annually."

With their four-pack carton aimed at the markets and chain stores and their syrups ready to move into fountains across the country, American Natural Beverage Corp. is poised for a major expansion. Soho, which had no advertising budget in 1984, had committed over $1 million to an advertising campaign for 1985–1986. Soho Natural Soda is rapidly moving forward with achieving greater national name recognition. "We had a real grass-roots effort," says Best. "We initially couldn't get into the big grocery chains because they didn't believe in natural soda." But adds Collier, "Soda is an intrinsic part of the American lifestyle, and we are the soft drink for the future."

JULIE BRICE

JULIE BRICE OF I CAN'T BELIEVE IT'S YOGURT

The key to a store's success is found in site selection. Every franchise applicant must submit at least three suggested sites. Brice foods will then study them, provide a computerized demographics study, and suggest the site that offers the optimal exposure to the target market.

In 1977, Julie Brice took over management of one of the two I Can't Believe It's Yogurt (ICBIY) stores in Dallas, Texas. Within a year she and her brother Bill had purchased the company and it had grown into a franchise conglomerate that currently has 100 stores in 25 states, eight of them company-owned. Two hundred are planned by year's end.

Now 27, Julie Brice, ICBIY's president, graduated as salutarian from Lakehill Preparatory School in Dallas, and cum laude from Southern Methodist University with a degree in business. While still attending Southern Methodist, Julie and Bill started working for a small frozen yogurt store close to campus. The original I Can't Believe It's Yogurt was having financial troubles, and the owners agreed to sell to their enterprising young managers. Studying full time at SMU, Julie and Bill worked daily at their store, often putting in 70 to 80 hours a week. "I learned so much more from my education," said Brice, "because I could take the tools and knowledge I was acquiring and apply them right away."

The Brices later developed their own secret yogurt recipe, ICBIY Softie®, which tastes just like ice cream. Compared with premium ice cream, the recipe contains 80 percent less fat, half the calories, and one-third more protein. ICBIY Softie® contains natural ingredients including whole milk from east Texas farms and yogurt cultures imported from Europe. In 1983, Julie and her brother built their own manufacturing facility, which is licensed to produce the ICBIY Softie®. I Can't Believe It's Yogurt stores offer French Vanilla and such unusual flavors as Chocolate Peach, Peanut Butter Fudge, Almond Amaretto, and Apple Pie. Toppings include fresh fruits, hot fudge, nuts, and candies. I Can't Believe It's Yogurt also offers a wide variety of shakes and "fruit smoothies," which are drinks of soft frozen yogurt blended with fruits and fruit juices.

Brice Foods, Inc., now the parent company for all her operations, markets Brice's Frozen Yogurt to supermarkets and chainstores throughout 30 states. Brice's frozen yogurt is sold in half-liter cartons to many of the major grocery chains, including Safeway, Skaggs, Big Star, Krogers, and Tom Thumb.

The Brice Foods plant, when in full production, is capable of producing 500,000 gallons of yogurt mix annually. The plant includes a testing facility for flavor and topping development. The company currently produces 19 different flavors of ICBIY Softie® and eight flavors of Brice Frozen Yogurt.

I Can't Believe It's Yogurt, Inc. company charges a franchise fee of $20,000 per store and a royalty of 6 percent of the gross sales, one-sixth of which is dedicated to the development of marketing materials for systemwide use. I Can't Believe It's Yogurt also offers "Master Development Franchise Agreements" which grant the rights to develop a number of stores within a state or specified region. I Can't Believe It's Yogurt offers an intensive ten-day training program for new franchise owners and keeps them updated through a team of field consultants and communication tools such as their newsletter "The Yogurt Scoop." In addition to providing classroom and on-site training for the owner and store manager, ICBIY offers guidance in site selection, public relations and advertising, accounting, and all facets of store operation.

According to Brice, one of the keys to a store's success is found in site selection. Every franchise applicant must submit at least three suggested sites. ICBIY will then visit and study the sites, and suggest the site that offers the optimal exposure to the target market. This is predominantly young, health-minded, above-average-income women. Women account for more than 60 percent of I Can't Believe It's Yogurt sales. On average, each yogurt store will produce over $200,000 in annual sales.

Brice is a strong believer in developing the company's growth through franchising. According to a U.S. Department of Commerce study, franchising is the fastest growing segment of the retail business. Franchising sales accounted for $529 billion in 1985, which was a 19 percent increase over last year. *Success Magazine* stated that by 1990 Americans will spend 45 cents out of every dollar eating out and that franchised food stores will continue to make up a growing part of the market. Ms. Brice specifically believes that health-related franchises, such as frozen yogurt stores, will enjoy an even greater percentage of the franchise food sales growth because "more people are becoming health conscious today. They are becoming more concerned about what they eat." The parent company, Brice Foods, Inc., had systemwide revenues of over $10 million in 1985, and Brice anticipated systemwide revenues of $17 million in 1986.

Brice is always testing new ideas both for her current franchises and for developing new ones. Recently, she and her brother opened Crumbles Cookie Kitchen, next to one of their yogurt stores in Dallas, to test her new cookie concept. Fut there is much more to Brice than just her business success. An active single woman, Brice swims for the Dallas-based Lone Star Masters swim team and competes in distance cycling events of 100 kilometers to 100 miles. She loves adventure and overseas traveling is her favorite pasttime. She actively supports the March of Dimes, the American Heart Association, and the Dallas group that supports the local arts. She believes that the quality she puts into her product and her stores is a great investment. Her continued support of her favorite charities and the community also provide her with personal satisfaction. Perhaps it is time to move over, Mrs. Fields.

JAMES CALANO AND JEFF SALZMAN

JAMES CALANO
AND JEFF SALZMAN
OF CAREERTRACK

"We can afford to offer these seminars for forty-five to ninety-five dollars per person. We may only break even, or even lose money on the seminars, but we make our profits on the back end, selling books, tapes, future private seminars, and even our mailing lists."

James Calano and Jeff Salzman came to the realization that there were no effective training courses where people could learn how to manage their careers when they felt the need for such a service in their own lives. Calano had previously been fired from his first professional job, and Salzman, unsatisfied and unfulfilled with his previous position, set out to wander around the country for a few years. They then discovered their own road to riches by running seminars that helped people think through what they want in their careers and how to achieve it.

"I guess my turn for the worse really turned out for the best," says Calano. Being fired from his previous job forced him to go into business for himself. "I set up shop in my second bedroom and declared myself in business," he says. He later took on Jeff Salzman as a partner. Calano today is president of CareerTrack, a company that he built from his bedroom into an organization that employs over 140 people.

When Calano and Salzman started CareerTrack at 24 and 28, respectively, first-year sales were $220,000. Their growth to date has been nothing short of phenomenal: $3.5 million in 1983, $5.4 million in 1984, $15 million is 1985, and a projected $25 million in 1986. Today, 29 and 32, Calano and Salzman share the privilege of operating a company that has grown to be the number one business seminar company in the industry. CareerTrack gave two thousand seminars last year to over 200,000 people in 350 cities in three countries: the United States, Canada, and Australia. Using *Inc.* Magazine's criteria for its list of the 100 fastest growing privately held companies in the United States, CareerTrack would be rated number 20.

What made CareerTrack such a unique success was Calano's and Salzman's understanding of the market. CareerTrack started by pricing their seminars at $45. Says Calano, "We gave more value at one-fourth the price. A lot of people price seminars according to their costs; we price our programs at what people can afford. We immediately stole market share."

CareerTrack hit a home run with its first seminar, which catered to the growing needs of the emerging women professionals. At a time when other seminar companies were folding due to the recession, when training budgets were among the first to be cut, CareerTrack hit paydirt because it found a growth market that had previously been untapped. CareerTrack's "Image and Self Projection" seminar for professional women, offered now in 350 cities, has taught women how to present themselves in business situations where both assertiveness and tact are important. The seminar advertises that success depends not only on how good you are, but how well you project how good you are to both your colleagues and your clients. Women often have trouble exercising power and assertiveness in certain business situations. This is usually due to societal norms rather than to any shortcomings in their abilities. CareerTrack retains a panel of successful professional women to present and prepare the seminars.

Other CareerTrack seminars include: "Achieving Excellence," "Getting Things Done," "How To Get Results With People," and "Stress Management of Professionals." CareerTrack also aggressively went after the corporate market. They provide over 500 on-site seminars a year to large corporations, including IBM, AT&T, 3M, General Motors, and Exxon. They also approached major government agencies— the army, the navy, the state department, the I.R.S., and the CIA. Their sales pitch succeeded with these clients because they could prove the immediate value of increased productivity as well as the advantage of being able to provide these seminars on location at reduced rates, thus saving the corporations and government agencies thousands of dollars in both seminar and travel fees.

Calano and Salzman are truly great promoters. They leveraged their firm's advertising budget by relying on all the free publicity they could create as opposed to simply paying for advertisements. They planned their seminars as media events in each city, garnering a lot of local newspaper coverage. They also established themselves with the publication of their first book *Real World 101*, published by Warner Books, which teaches college students "What College Never Taught You about Career Success." These words of wisdom are encased rather intriguingly in sections titled: "Body Snatchers, Head-Hunters and Flesh Peddlers," "When the Shit Hits the Fan," and "Kick-Ass Confidence." The book has sold more than 60,000 copies nationwide, and they are now working on their second book, *Success Short-Cuts*.

The seminar and training industry is today an over $4 billion industry. The reason for the growth in the professional training industry is best stated by Lee Iacocca in his book, *Iacocca*: "It's always a shame when a person with great talent can't tell the board or a committee what's in his or her head. More often than not, a course would make all the difference." Calano plans to capitalize on this need by becoming "the McDonald's of the training industry." Calano envisions future professional training stores across the country. "There'll be a kiosk in every mall," says Calano. "Our goal is $100 million in sales by 1988."

But with all these activities, Calano still takes time to serve as a Big Brother to a fatherless child, a contribution of his time that he has made for over 10 years. He spends three hours a week, every week, with his "little brother" and contributes to and participates in the activities of the executive committee for the Big Brothers of Colorado. "After all," says Calano, "true satisfaction is not derived by how many cars you can drive or how many suits you can wear. True satisfaction is found in succeeding in a business that you love, and helping people." He couldn't have said it better.

"IF YOU THINK THINGS ARE TOUGH HERE IN AMERICA, YOU SHOULD GO TO MY COUNTRY"— HUNGRY IMMIGRANT ENTREPRENEURS

When the first great wave of immigrants came to these shores in the late 1800s and early 1900s their lives were very hard, there was no welfare, no minimum wage, or social security. But they found jobs, worked hard, saved their money, and built the greatest nation that has ever evolved in modern history. My grandfather was one of those immigrants; he fled the religious persecution of Eastern Europe. He marveled at the opportunity provided by this young country, which gave

101

him the freedom both to worship as he chose and establish his own enterprise. Today we are quick to complain about how immigration is hurting our country rather than helping it, that present citizens are losing their jobs to the new arrivals, and that there is just not enough work to go around.

Many of our established labor unions have become quick to join this chorus of complaint about immigration. We have resorted to complaining and protectionism rather than ingenuity and independence. The fact of the matter is, if most of the Mexicans were sent back across the border, many of our farmers would never be able to find employees among our present ranks willing to help them harvest their crops. Restaurants and dozens of other service businesses would also be forced to close.

Is it harsh to suggest that recent immigrants fill a void in our employment sector where many latter-day generations of Americans refuse to work? No. Today, immigrants still have an important role to play in our society. Like my grandfather who was employed in tenement factories in New York's Lower East Side and later started his own business, many recent immigrants from Latin America and Asia work hard to provide vital goods and services. They scrimp and save to send their sons and daughters to college. Like my grandfather, they, too, believe in the American dream. In fact, many of our recent immigrants have founded companies that have provided thousands of jobs for other Americans. Companies like Wang, founded by Chinese immigrant An Wang, and Televideo Systems, founded by Korean immigrant Kyupin Philip Hwang.

Had we closed our doors to immigrants in the past, we would never have been able to enjoy the benefits that their hard work has brought us today. If we close our doors now, how many more future Einsteins will be turned away from our shores? How many more Wangs and Hwangs will be forced to set up their businesses overseas?

Immigration has been the lifeblood that infuses new vitality in American industry and society. It still is. No one knows and appreciates the value of our free society more than our new immigrants. Their industriousness and hard work remind us of the opportunity that still exists here. If you doubt my words, take a look at all the recent immigrants in cities like New York and Los Angeles who work long hours running small businesses, such as newspaper stands or grocery stores. Like my grandfather and father did, these immigrants encourage their children to work in the stores alongside their parents. The industriousness is passed on to their children at an early age.

On a recent trip to Great Britain I attended a government-supported class on new enterprise at which I was invited to speak. I was shocked to hear the very students enrolled in the new enterprise class railing at me for my capitalist views and indignant about the fact that they couldn't get the capital to start their businesses because the government would not provide them with the funds to establish the new enterprises. Many of the students admitted that they or their families were currently on "the dole" (unemployment welfare payments) and believed that they had no hope of getting jobs. The only student in the class who openly sided with my views was an Indian immigrant who worked in his father's shop and planned to open his own. Privately the other students attacked the "bastards who come over here" to take away their jobs. As you know, the socialist-leaning economy of Britain has not fared too well recently; should we start speaking and thinking the same, the same fate will probably fall upon us.

Let us never forget our ingenuity and ambition, or the freedom and opportunity that this country provides. Let us never forget the feeling of hunger in our bellies that spurs us on to achieve. Should we ever forget that feeling we need only look to our immigrant entrepreneurs, for their feeling of hunger is still fresh from the experience of their previous country.

JAY ADONI

JAY ADONI OF ADMOS SHOE CORPORATION

"Everybody in America is worried about the Asians and Latin Americans outselling them in price and the Europeans outselling them in style." Adoni's secret is that he constantly offers his customers an array of new styles. "My guys can be in a shoe store in Italy on Monday, be back in the factory with photographers on Tuesday, and have a few shoes in the salesman's hands on Wednesday. . . .

In 1976, 17-year-old Jay Adoni emigrated to America with $20 in his pocket. His climb from a shoe factory shipping clerk to the owner of a shoe manufacturing company, employing over 250 people and in 1986 grossing over $20 million in sales, seems more like a story about the American immigrants of a century ago. "It can still happen in this country," says Adoni, "but you have to be willing to work hard, real hard." Adoni, now 27, who came from Israel unable to speak English and with nothing more than his ambition and his $20, did just that—he worked very hard. In an industry where the United States seemed to have all but lost out to competition from Latin America and Asian countries where labor was cheap, Adoni has, in just a few short years, been able to show a growth record that would be impressive in any industry. "My competitors just don't know how I do it; they are all busy shutting down their factories and I'm busy expanding and buying their equipment and inventory at the liquidation sales," says Adoni. "Why, what's the matter with you? You don't think that I bought any of this equipment and machines brand new, at full price, do you?"

In the October 7, 1985 issue of *Time* magazine, an article entitled "Three Industries That Want Help" concluded that "the U.S. Shoe Industry seems beyond saving." Seymour Fabri, president of the Southern California Shoe Manufacturers Association, is quoted as saying, "The shoe industry is doomed." "The American shoe makers just got lazy," says Adoni with a shrug. "Everybody in America is worried about the Asians and Latin Americans outselling them in price and the Europeans outselling them in style. For an American shoe company to succeed, you got to be able to move fast to notice the new hot styles, quickly produce them, and provide them to your customers." Adoni's secret is that he constantly offers his customers an array of new styles. He and his staff travel often to Europe and constantly keep on top of the fashion trends. "My guys can be in a shoe store in Italy on Monday, be back in the factory with photographers on Tuesday, and have a few shoes in the salesman's hands on Wednesday," proclaims Adoni. "Hell, we even knock off the Asians. We're probably the only group in America that they have to worry is going to copy their ideas and compete with them."

"The women's shoe market loves diversity in fashion and design. The key to sales growth is constantly providing the market with what's new and exciting. If a woman sees something new and exciting in a shoe store, she'll buy it. But she won't buy if she already has a pair like it in the closet." With this strategy Adoni has developed and maintained a list of satisfied customers that includes Nordstrom's, Bloomingdale's, Macy's, Bullock's, and Dayton Hudson.

Adoni is proud of the fact that he can slug it out with the overseas producers and succeed when many other American shoe manufacturers have thrown in the towel. It makes a case for why new immigrants have been the life blood to building the American economy. They come here filled with ambition and willing to work hard. They're hungry and they won't let foreign competition threaten them; rather, they would prefer to make threats of their own. "If you think staying in business here is tough, you should try it in Israel. Things are much better here by comparison." Says Adoni, "I don't mind working hard, I never complain—working hard has brought me a big house and nice car and lovely family; I got everything I want."

While it's clear that although that statement may apply to Adoni's personal life, it is in no way characteristic of his business attitude. Adoni isn't satisfied with just maintaining his sales growth. "We want to go to thirty or forty million dollars soon," he says. "We built a twenty million dollar business with start-up capital of just fifteen thousand dollars. Perhaps now we might consider invested capital to take us to the next stage of growth, so forty million dollars in sales won't take as long as twenty million did."

While MBA programs warn young entrepreneurial hopefuls that they shouldn't dream of launching a new company without start-up venture capital of $1 million or more, Adoni has proved that it ain't necessarily so. He has followed in the footsteps of the entrepreneurs who came to these shores in the last two centuries, before venture capital became fashionable, and like them, he started with nothing and built his company up by sweat. But working and growing without a capital base has had its hardships. Jay may own a lot larger share of his company than other founders who had outside investors have had, but it comes at a high price. The company has to pay over $500,000 a year to banks for factoring services and interest and financing fees. "If we had invested capital to finance our own receivables, that $500,000 would easily be added into our bottom line each year," he says.

To date Adoni has no outside investors. He has taken on two working partners, his brother-in-law, Lance Rubin, who is the chief designer, and his sales manager, Larry Kriedman. Getting these three guys to sit still together in a room is like walking into a hornets' nest and asking the hornets to listen to you. The phone never stops ringing, and whether it's a major client calling or one of the employees who has a problem fixing a machine, Jay, Lance, and Larry are either on the phone or underneath the machine with wrench in hand. Jay hates sitting down in his office for a long period of time. He prefers to walk the factory floor regularly. The employees love to see him. "Many of these guys started with me almost six years ago when I was just beginning in a one-room shop. They think I'm God now. They are like family to me, and I'm responsible for all their families."

Many of Adoni's employees are recent immigrants themselves. In his factory, located in the Greenpoint section of Brooklyn, a visitor is greeted at the door by the receptionist, who recently emigrated from Poland. As you walk in the office you'll notice the Chinese bookkeepers, who rarely raise their heads from their ledgers. On the factory floor, which is kept spotless, you'll notice the proud Puerto Rican and other Latin American factory foremen instructing the new sewing machine operators in Spanish. "I counted it once, I think there are more than five or six languages spoken here. It's a wonder how we all communicate so well," says Adoni.

Adoni's success has enabled him to help his family overseas, who are of modest means. He introduced his brother, who he says he has recently "imported from Israel." "I imported him because Lance needed some help in the design department, so my brother is helping out and they work real well together."

Adoni is currently buying the building that houses his 40,000-square-foot factory. He has so far arranged for an Industrial Revenue Bond to finance the $2.1 million purchase price. The borough of Brooklyn has been more than happy to provide the bond because the business has generated many new jobs.

Another recent achievement is a partnership he formed with a Brazilian shoe manufacturer to produce very intricate and labor-intensive shoes that require hand weaving. Their chief sales manager, Larry Kriedman, has made dozens of trips to Brazil and claims "these guys are great at knocking out the hot new styles that require a lot of hard work at a low price." He waves a moccasin. "See this? This is going to sell like hotcakes this year—the art deco hand-weaving is great. I always keep this style shoe on me, I even sleep with it under my pillow. I am going to sell the hell out of it this year. Right now you're looking at our next million dollars of new sales." Admos also will use its Brazilian partnership to import a hot new line of colorful "fun fashion" shoes called "Video," which they expect to be a big winner this year. Jay also has plans to expand his main brand line, which he produces under the label "L.J. Simone, New York."

Their only regrets are, as Lance says: "Running this business and growing so fast has required a big lifestyle change. I loved to read science fiction novels and take vacations; now

I can't even take the time to buy a book." Larry has to force himself to be back for the holidays between trips to Brazil. But they agree with Jay: "We work hard, but we have no real complaints. How can you complain too much when you are making money while watching your competition close their doors?"

THOMAS C. K. YUEN, SAFI V. QURESHEY,
AND ALBERT C. WONG

QURESHEY, WONG, AND YUEN OF AST RESEARCH, INC.

Qureshey drew parallels between the PC industry today and the automobile industry during its inception. . . . There was (and is) the obvious opportunity to enhance the performance of a basic black Model T (plain-vanilla PC) with engine accessories and higher octane fuels (expanded memory, mass storage, graphics). But beyond that, automobiles created a whole new demand for paved city streets (local area networks), expressways (micro-to-mini/ mainframe data links), and interstate highways (telecommunication facilities)."

In June of 1980, three immigrant engineers banded together to establish a new company to manufacture accessories for the personal computer. They knew success would be a long shot. The odds were that of the thousands of pairs and trios tinkering in their garages, few would ever evolve into successful high-growth companies. But their dream was one that they would not give up. They believed in their product and felt sure they had found a niche in the market, a need that had to be filled. They knew that venture capitalists would shun them, so they hired out as consultants to pay their bills and borrowed $50,000 for investment capital by taking out second mortgages on their homes. They quickly learned finance, high volume manufacturing, and controlled growth. And their growth was nothing short of phenomenal. In just five years their company, AST Research, had sales that have grown from $71,000 in 1981 to close to $140 million in 1986, representing an annual growth rate of 657 percent. Net income has grown over the past three years at a compounded annual growth rate of 244 percent, with AST reporting a profit of $19 million at the close of fiscal year 1985.

The three founders started their business on a shoestring budget in their mid to late 20s. Now in their 30s, they each have a net worth in excess of $40 million. All three are testimony that America still provides a great opportunity for success for recent immigrants today as it did over a century ago. The past generations came from Europe; AST's founders are modern day immigrants from the Far East. Although the countries from which they come are different, the dreams of coming to America are the same.

Safi Qureshey, AST's president, is originally from Pakistan, Albert Wong, executive vice president of technical development, and Thomas Yuen, executive vice president of strategic planning, are both recent immigrants from Hong Kong. The essence of the company has remained very much the same, a partnership built on friendship and equality amongst three young men who run their business by talking things over, as if they were still back in the garage.

AST's birthplace was a garage in Santa Ana, California. The members initially held down jobs or consulting positions during the day and worked on the new products at night. Often, members of Wong's family pitched in, stuffing circuit boards to assist the fledgling enterprise before it could hire employees. Their start-up operation was a far cry from a cookbook MBA case study. They had no business plan, very little management experience, and no venture capital financing other than the small amount they could scrape up by refinancing their homes. But perhaps what they did have was even more important, a bright idea for a needed innovation, a perceptive understanding of the marketplace, and the personal determination and perseverance to carry out their plans.

AST's products are personal computer enhancement products that increase a PC's performance capabilities, such as increased speed, memory, and communications capabilities. The founders saw a large installed base of personal computers that were becoming more and more obsolete every day due to the rapid advancements in speed, memory, and networking capabilities being provided in newer models. Qureshey, Wong, and Yuen bet that, rather than having to replace their computers every six months, people would prefer to have an alternative to purchase add-on products that would upgrade their PC's capabilities to present day state-of-the-art standards. Says Qureshey, "PCs are becoming the typewriters of the future . . . with over 4 million IBM PC's already installed, we have a huge market for our products."

AST's strategy is based on designing products that complement IBM PCs rather than trying to compete against them.

They help upgrade older model PCs to new, more advanced capabilities at a fraction of the replacement cost. AST is a manufacturer of board-level enhancement products and is becoming a growing force within the areas of data communications, local area networks (LAN), and graphic products. It relies heavily on research and development in order to keep ahead of its competition. A number of other companies have joined the ranks of computer upgrade purveyors since the AST's establishment, so the founders have yet to slow down.

What the company calls "multifunction board products" accounted for 82 percent of its sales last year. These products combine several features, such as increased memory and input/output functions, on one circuit board. Some of the hottest sellers on its product line include SIXPAK-PLUS®, Advantage®, and Rampage!®. IBM has selected a number of AST products to offer through its Product Centers.

But AST did not stop with IBM products; it also manufactures upgrades for Apple as well as for other manufacturers. In 1985 AST reached an agreement with Sears to sell AST products through Sears' 105 Business Systems Centers throughout the United States. AST also sells to Computerland, Businessland, IBM Product Centers and Entre Computer Stores.

The company now has worldwide distribution, with subsidiaries based in the United Kingdom and Asia. AST is aggressively pursuing sales overseas as well as domestically. It has shifted some of the product production to Hong Kong in order to maintain price competitiveness with foreign-based manufacturers. A key to the company's continued success is that it could see the need and enter the market early in order to establish the all-important brand name recognition so important in this part of the computer industry for continued sales growth. AST constantly watches for needed innovation and support products, which are developed when new PC products are released. "Any announcement that IBM makes brings on opportunities for us," says Yuen. When IBM announced the production of its communication systems that allowed PCs access to its mainframes by PCs, but did not provide for linking up mainframe files to the PC's printer, AST responded immediately with products developed to provide printer support.

In a letter to shareholders in AST's most recent annual report, Safi Qureshey drew parallels between the PC industry today and the automobile industry during its inception. "Then, as now, a mass-produced, aggressively marketed high tech product revolutionized our economy and society. Then, as now, brand new industries and major new companies burst into being in the wake of the new technology. There was (and is) the obvious opportunity to enhance the performance of a basic black Model T (plain-vanilla PC) with engine accessories and higher octane fuels (expanded memory, mass storage, graphics). But beyond that, automobiles created a whole new demand for paved city streets (LANs), expressways (micro-to-mini/mainframe data links), and interstate highways (telecommunication facilities)."

AST's plans for the future are to continue to expand its product lines to capitalize on new needs and developments that are created within the PC industry. Says Qureshey: "As a company, AST has always taken the position that in the long run, success cannot be based on products, but on the people who create, make, and market those products. Despite its rapid growth, AST has managed to retain its entrepreneurial spirit on all levels. It is on this sense of urgency and enthusiasm that we base our optimistic hopes for the future."

FINDING A NEED AND FILLING IT— OPPORTUNITIES CREATED IN HIGH TECHNOLOGY

Previous chapters covered a few dynamos engaged in high tech businesses. Protocom Devices founder, Raphael Collado, saw a need for different computer systems to be able to communicate with each other. He filled the need by creating a device that made this possible. SUN Microsystems' Scott McNealy recognized a need for "a better mousetrap." He founded SUN to create a more efficient and cost-effective CAD/CAM system in order to compete with existing manufacturers. Steve Kirsch's innovation was literally to "build a better mouse," and entrepreneurs Yuen, Wong, and Qureshey capitalized on the opportunity that existed in providing add-on products so that existing PCs could be updated to the capabilities of newer models.

All the high tech innovators cannot be confined to one section because their stories do overlap on some other very important points. Like all entrepreneurs, the technical innovators have to learn the lessons common to all businesses. What makes their particular businesses unique or different is in part the glamour currently associated with high technology business activities and the lightning speed at which great new opportunities are created in this arena.

Part of the evolution from an industrial to an advanced technology or information society has created opportunities for young people to head businesses making millions, and even billions, at ages that would not be possible in previous decades. Apple Computer became a member of the Fortune 500 before either founding partner reached the age of 30; this would have been almost unthinkable less than 20 years ago. The personal computer appeared on the horizon less than 10 years ago, and already it has become a multibillion-dollar industry.

Every technical advance and innovation creates new opportunities, both within the industries themselves and for new businesses providing products or services to support these new industries. Because these markets move very fast, the high technology game incorporates high risks as well as high returns. However, bold entrepreneurs with foresight can reap great benefits from meeting the challenge.

In the chapters to follow we will see how Philippe Kahn established his business and proved the industry experts wrong by providing advanced software for a market he saw as more sophisticated than the "experts" realized. Kahn saw the need to provide PC users with quality, affordable software. In filling that need he broke all the established rules by offering his first products at a low $49.95.

Similarly, Michael Dell realized that brand name affiliation for personal computers will soon go the way of designer jeans. As the market became more sophisticated, people were more interested in paying for power and function than for the label on the terminal. He offered the public the alternative of buying his computer system direct from the manufacturer at one-third the brand-name competitor's cost. Gary Steele's company, on the other hand, was not founded to provide a lower cost competitive product. Rather, Molecular Devices was created to produce a revolutionary technical innovation that has the potential for major advances in the medical industry.

PHILIPPE KAHN

PHILIPPE KAHN
OF BORLAND
INTERNATIONAL

"We're not greedy. We believe that it is better to sell hundreds of thousands of software programs at a reasonable price instead of a few at prices that would make Jesse James blush."

The company does not rely on any one product to produce more than 20 percent of its revenues. Offering a variety of well-designed and useful products is Borland's key to continued growth.

"We never started this company with the intention of becoming millionaires in Silicon Valley," says Philippe Kahn, founder and president of Borland International. "We just wanted to have fun and make new products that we believe in." With that philosophy, Kahn, who had arrived in the United States in 1982 with just $2,000, created one of the most innovative and successful computer software companies in the country. Indeed, Borland is perhaps one of the fastest growing software companies in the world.

In his early 20s, Kahn studied under Niklaus Wirth, noted author of the Pascal programming language, at ETH University in Zurich, Switzerland. He spent a number of years after graduation as a mathematics professor in his native France, at Nice and Grenoble. At the age of 30, Kahn came to the United States to witness "Silicon Valley fever" first-hand. With an innovative new software product, Turbo Pascal, under his arm, he knocked on the doors of the major software companies and venture capital firms looking for backers for his development ideas. But the conventional wisdom of established software publishers kept them from seeing the market potential for "another version of Pascal," particularly when they heard of Kahn's plans to introduce his program through mail order at a quarter of the price of competitive ones. Most industry experts told Kahn they didn't see a market greater than 40,000 unit sales for Pascal development software. Undaunted, Kahn released his first product in November of 1983 and sold more than 25,000 copies of Turbo Pascal by mail order within the first month. Turbo Pascal was later chosen by *PC Week* as product of the year for offering users the highest performance programming tool on the market. The company followed the Turbo Pascal product with a string of complementary programming toolboxes.

According to Kahn, "It's easy to have an idea; it's another thing to make it work." Kahn's idea was to offer high-quality, easy-to-use software at affordable prices. Consequently, all Borland's products to date range in price from $50 to $150 per software package. The company works on the principle that selling a great product at a fair price will mean that people will continue to buy from you, rather than devise a way to copy your product. Borland's strategy is simple, says Vice President of Business Development, Spencer Leyton. "It costs $69 to buy a copy of Turbo Pascal and $73 to Xerox the manual."

Leyton, who joined Borland a year ago after serving as director of product services at Softsel, a major Los Angeles software distributor (and now a Borland customer), recalls the days when "Philippe first convinced me to pick up his products." Says Leyton, "I kept getting mock-threatening messages on my desk from sales reps, saying, 'If you value your life, pick up Turbo Pascal,' or, 'Pick up Turbo Pascal or don't start your car.'" Leyton signed an agreement with Borland a few months later and then joined the company. Says Leyton, "We plan to be to software what Kodak is to photography."

In June of 1984, Borland unleashed its second major product, SideKick, which became the standard in RAM-resident desktop organization software. SideKick, which was originally developed for internal use by the Borland staff, is a highly efficient desktop organizer that includes a notepad, calendar, calculator, and automatic phone dialer, all for only $84.95 without copy protection. It became the standard in RAM-resident desktop organization software.

The company was later to follow with a string of software successes. In late September of 1985 Borland added another product to its list, Reflex, the Analyst. Reflex is an advanced data analysis program that Borland acquired from Analytica, a start-up software manufacturer. Borland is selling the highly regarded product for $149.95.

But perhaps the company's most outstanding development is one of their latest releases, Turbo Lightning. Turbo Lightning has had an explosive impact on the software industry. To quote the December 10, 1985 cover story of *PC Magazine*, "Lightning is a revolution in the making and revolution is a word *PC Magazine* has scrupulously tried to avoid for two years." Lightning is an instant electronic information access and retrieval system and reference library for personal computers. It currently includes the 83,000-word Random House Concise Spelling Dictionary and the 50,000-word Random House Thesaurus. Planned libraries include dictionaries and encyclopedias for specific professions, such as accounting, medicine, real estate, and history. Lightning is compatible with many widely used software programs. A recent addition to the Turbo Lightning Library is the Word Wizard, a development toolbox that serves as a technical reference manual with on-line examples and also includes four word games.

In April 1986 Borland introduced Turbo Prolog, a fifth generation artificial intelligence language development system. Turbo Prolog takes the PC a step beyond its traditional computing functions. It is a declarative language and therefore has the ability to infer or derive information from stated facts. It can be used for powerful applications, such as customized knowledge bases known as "expert systems" and "smart" information management systems.

Borland's leading-edge developments have enabled it to become the fifth largest software manufacturer in the United States. Kahn has seen his staff grow from 4 to 160 in less than three years. Sales grew from an estimated $200,000 in 1983 to $30 million in 1985, and industry analysts project 1986 sales at more than $50 million. Borland has come a long way from its early days above an automotive repair shop. Kahn quips, "Some companies got their start in a garage. We started *above* the garage!" Borland currently maintains its modern headquarters in Scotts Valley, California, with other offices in the United Kingdom and Europe.

Kahn is undoubtedly an industry iconoclast. His views are strong and well defined, and his new programs often prove how obsolete conventional industry philosophy is. According to Kahn, "Good software is not created by committee, it is done by a small group of people." He feels that the industry has been continuously overpricing its products, and his company reflects that viewpoint in its advertisements: "We're not greedy. We believe that it is better to sell hundreds of thousands of software programs at a reasonable price instead of a few at prices that would make Jesse James blush."

Kahn is a firm believer in individual creativity. He doesn't believe that "great software companies are created solely by pin stripers with MBAs." Says Kahn: "It takes hands-on knowledge of what goes on between people and computers. The difficult thing to find is not money but the right people." That philosophy has allowed Borland to maintain its independent nature and Kahn to attract some of the best creative technical and marketing talent from around the world.

Kahn envisions Borland as becoming a software publishing house of the future. He believes Borland's strength lies in the fact that unlike many of its competitors, the company does not rely on any one product to produce more than 20 percent of its revenues. Offering a variety of well-designed and useful products is Borland's key to continued growth.

The day may come when we find Borland products becoming a part of our everyday lives. But although Borland may very well have that future in mind, Kahn emphasizes that his most important goal for Borland is "to continue to be a fun place to work."

MICHAEL DELL

MICHAEL DELL OF PC'S LIMITED

A key word that keeps coming up in discussions about PC's Limited is "determination." "I opened my first store literally six days before final exams as a pre-med student. A lot of people thought I was crazy, but I was determined to do it and nothing was going to stop me."

PC's Limited is a national force in manufacturing and in the direct-relationship marketing of microcomputers and related products. The story of how the company has risen to prominence in less than two-and-one-half years is a testimony to the workings of the American free market system, which always accommodates a player with a new slant and a better idea. Michael Dell, the 21-year-old founder and CEO, is a modern day Horatio Alger, who would probably give old Horatio a run for his money. Within two years, Dell has succeeded in building an $80 million company. Even more fascinating is that he did it with no outside investments or venture capital, and he still owns 100 percent of the company.

PC's Limited was established in early 1984 when Dell, a premed student at the University of Texas at Austin, decided that he had the marketing and merchandising skills to make a living selling IBM PCs and related products, such as hard disks and printers, at deep discounts. Initially, Dell started with only $18,000 in personal savings and relied on small advertisements in the Austin newspaper. But soon he decided to go nationwide and contracted with a local advertising agency to place ads in trade publications such as *PC Week* and *Byte*. Within a few months, he had outgrown his university-area apartment and moved into a small office retail store. By steadily increasing his advertising budget, employee roster, and inventory, Dell began making substantial strides.

Two moves—the first to a 2,350-square-foot office and the second into one more than three times as large, which itself was later expanded into an adjoining 6,000-square-foot warehouse—were the next two milestones in the development of PC's Limited. At this time, October of 1984, Dell was able to start serious work on designing and building his own machines. Dell never intended to be just another reseller of merchandise. That was how he got his start, but it was just a means to an end. He reached his goal of producing his own computer in mid-1985, when PC's Limited introduced the Turbo PC. It sold for $795 and ran 40 percent faster than the IBM PC, the industry standard at that time.

Reaction to the new machine in the trade press was overwhelming. Jim Seymour of *PC Week* remarked, "A fine box. One I'd happily choose over Big Blue's original." *MIS Week* exclaimed, "It almost sounds unbelievable." The company was instantly swamped with orders, some for 100 or more units. Actually, many of the first volume buyers were "full price" retailers who bought the machine from PC's Limited and resold it at a markup under its own label.

The Turbo PC was followed by PC's Limited 2868, which also offered superior performance to the IBM industry standard at less cost. Again the industry press gave PC's Limited a standing ovation. "The PC's Limited 2868 proved to be the functional equivalent to the IBM product, only faster. Priced at roughly one-third less, it rates as one of the best bargains available," stated Winn Rosch in *PC Magazine*. In the PC article Rosch added, "It's enough to make you think hard about crossing the IBM AT—or even XT—off your purchase order and inking in PC's Limited 2868." Further on in his article, Rosch went on to say, "According to Michael Dell, the 20-year-old president of PC's Limited, he's gotten a few of his machines up to 10 MHz. When I was 20, I was still trying to figure out what girls were." Since the time that review was written, Dell has produced 12 and 16 MHz machines.

By this time, Dell and his management staff realized that with an overwhelming crush of orders and a staff that was approaching 80 full-timers, new space was needed immediately. Through a fortunate circumstance, a newly constructed building in north Austin became available that looked as though it had been specifically designed for the young company's needs. Soon after, PC's Limited moved into its new 30,000-square-foot headquarters and underwent significant expansion. Dell developed manufacturing agreements with companies in Taiwan and Japan that furthered their rapid growth. More recently, Dell acquired space in an 80,000-square-foot manufacturing facility, which is near the head-quarters building.

To Dell, it seems as if only yesterday he was keeping track of incoming orders by hanging them up with clothespins on a wire that ran the length of his office wall. Dell wouldn't leave his office until all of the orders that day were pulled off the clothespins, packed, and shipped down to UPS. "I started realizing that we were really a growing company when UPS would come to our office for pickups. Pretty soon we were filling two or three trucks a day." Dell says there is no secret to his company's rapid growth. "We consistently offered a better product at a better price and we worked hard. In fact, we worked 14-hour days, seven days a week." People would ask Dell what time he would close his store and Dell would always respond, "We close when we fall down."

A key word that keeps coming up in discussions about PC's Limited is "determination." Says Dell, I literally opened my first store six days before final exams. A lot of people thought I was crazy, but I was determined to do it and nothing was going to stop me." Dell finished his first year at the University of Texas and then went into designing new products full time for his growing new business. Dell was determined to prove that PC's Limited was a solid company that not only offered the best products but would stand behind each product shipped. He offered an unconditional 30-day money-back guarantee on all its products. "I think that really says something about PC's Limited, primarily that we're honest and ethical people—not a fly-by-night company. We are definitely here to stay," says Dell.

PC's Limited is known as a technological leader among direct-relationship marketers. The company's aggressively discounted pricing has been maintained by selling directly to the consumer through direct response advertising and to major corporations via company sales staff. This has eliminated costly multilevel markups that would have resulted from selling through dealers, distributors, and retailers. PC's Limited also reduces its sales cost by not competing with the major manufacturers' advertising budgets. Rather than relying on major television and magazine advertisements to sell its machines, the company believes that offering a better machine at one-half to one-third the cost is a greater factor than expensive advertising in determining the customer's purchase. There will always be stiff competition, especially in sales to status seekers who require a national brand name. But as Jim Seymour of *PC Week* put it, "There's no status in buying a few dozen generic PC's—beyond the status that attaches to getting twice as much for your money."

For a 21-year-old corporate CEO, Dell seems to have management expertise far beyond his years. "I like to think the people I have under me can do their jobs independently of me and make all their own decisions, be held accountable for their own mistakes and be rewarded for their achievements." Dell transmits his own enthusiasm to all his employees and believes everyone should feel that their job is important and meaningful to the company. The team spirit he has fostered has led to the employees' desire to attend Dell's informal classes on new products, including secretaries and receptionists. "If everyone in the company senses the quality and value of our products and the exciting things that we're doing, soon that excitement will be transmitted to everyone who comes in contact with us," says Dell.

PC's Limited now employs more than 250 full-time professionals, ranging from marketing and sales representatives to engineers and programmers, to assembly personnel, to corporate management.

PC's Limited has become a major vendor to many of the Fortune 2,000 buyers in the country and sells its products worldwide. Major clients include Price Waterhouse, Arthur Anderson, Ashton Tate, Martin Marietta, and the universities of Arizona, California, and Texas. Thanks to ongoing research and development efforts, the company now offers a wide range of "house brand" products, including add-on boards, modems, hard drives, monitors, and the computers previously mentioned.

As an indication of just how interested the market is in the firm and its products, at the Fall 1985 COMDEX trade show, in spite of having a large-scale booth, PC's Limited was overwhelmed by retailers wishing to market its computers. In addition, interviews of Dell and other key executives at the trade show brought excellent publicity to the company.

With a current advertising budget topping $2.6 million and sales for the current year estimated at more than $80 million, PC's Limited has achieved major recognition in the marketplace. Dell currently has a staff of top research and development professionals working on products that will make even greater breakthroughs in the microcomputer world. The company is poised to ride the crest of the demand for price and performance in microcomputer equipment.

If Dell's own personal interest is any indication of the future direction of the company, it is clear the company will continue to emphasize engineering and development. "What I really like to do," says Dell, "is to develop a new product and collaborate with engineers in bringing it to fruition." As for the nature of his future products, Dell remarks, "More speed, more smarts, more of what the customer wants." PC's Limited is dedicated to maintaining its position as a market leader in direct marketing of state-of-the-art technology at discount prices. "We'll always have hardware to support the latest and greatest technology at the best value—no matter what it is, UNIX or MS/DOS. We watch the market closely, and we'll always be there ahead of the other guy at a better price." The future success of PC's Limited should be as clear as this author's decision about where to buy his next personal computer.

GARY STEELE

GARY STEELE OF MOLECULAR DEVICES CORPORATION

"I have always said that when I grew up I wanted to run something."

After completing his MBA at Stanford University and serving five years with the prestigious management consulting firm of McKinsey & Co. (where his co-workers were Tom Peters and Robert Waterman of *In Search of Excellence* fame) Gary Steele exchanged the security of that position for a high-risk entrepreneurial venture. He joined Genentech, a California-based genetic engineering firm then in its early stages. As vice president of product development, Steele helped the company grow to its current world renown.

Gary Steele was a success in every respect. He first proved his ability to succeed in the big corporate world; he took a risk and proved his ability to help lead an entrepreneurial high tech company. Why, then, did he quit his successful and established position with Genentech to join another high-risk start-up venture? "I have always said that when I grew up I wanted to run something," Steele explains. "One day I got a phone call from a headhunter whose client was Molecular Devices. The company was in its formative stages then, and they needed a president to run it. When I learned more about the company, I knew this was the right opportunity."

According to Steele, now 38, what Molecular Devices is doing is "linking the world of solid state microelectronics and biochemistry." Steele claims that the company is creating a revolution in both industries through its development of a new silicon-based biosensor chip that can be used to provide real-time on-site testing of biological samples, such as blood and urine, for the diagnosis of disease. The prototypes are under development. If successful, Molecular Devices will be the first company to develop stable biosensors that can be used for diagnosing a full range of diseases. "In layman terms," says Steele, "we have succeeded in getting biological material to talk directly to stable electronic devices for directly measuring molecules in human, animal, food, and soil samples." More important, the system will provide doctors, hospitals, and even people in their homes or soldiers in the field with immediate diagnosis, and it will aid in selecting the proper prescription to treat the ailment. No longer will physicians have to send samples to outside labs for analysis, with the resultant lapse of days or weeks before treatment. This efficient system will deliver the information to the doctor promptly and cost-effectively.

Steele gives credit to Dr. Hardin McConnell, professor of physical chemistry at Stanford University, and the scientists at Molecular Devices for developing the system. The Sutter Hill venture capital firm of Menlo Park, California, and Schering Plough Corp. provided the initial financing for Molecular Devices. Steele expects to be able to produce and sell the product within one year. Steele refers to Molecular Devices as "a classic Silicon Valley high tech venture." "The only difference," he adds, "is that in this day and age, where everyone is having a hard time raising money, we were able to raise ample funds from a strong group of backers before even writing a formal business plan."

Molecular Devices has grown in eight months from an initial group of five people to a current staff of 28. Steele expects to have 34 employees before the year is over.

Steele believes that there is a formula for running and building a successful small company, focused on three key points:

1. *Hire and keep the very best and brightest.* Steele emphasizes the importance of this. "I am the head of recruiting— I don't delegate that." Steele encourages the advantage of employee stock options as an excellent way to attract *and keep* good people.

2. *Set goals and milestones with clear underlying assumptions.* Track and report progress against a set of ag-

gressive but achievable goals and milestones. People must clearly understand the assumptions underlying these goals and milestones. If assumptions change, quickly revisit the goals and see if they remain achievable. "A lot of people talk about this," says Steele, "but very few actually do it."

3. *Be resourceful.* A small company cannot compete with a big company on the basis of resources. Small companies must find the equalizers by playing smarter and by working harder with the limited resources that they have. Small companies can't afford people with big-company mentalities who cannot adapt to not having big budgets and large staffs. Small companies need creative people who know how to make the most of what they have.

Steele claims that there is even a formula for leadership in a small company. "Leadership equals Salesmanship." The selling of ideas, concepts, values, and beliefs is what makes a leader.

Steele should know, in a survey of peers in the San Francisco area, Steele was recently recognized as one of the 12 rising stars of Silicon Valley who could most affect change.

MAKING IT BIG IN REAL ESTATE

There are more than 2.2 million licensed real estate professionals in the United States. They range from brokers to leasing agents. While there are examples of very successful brokers who make large sums of money in annual commissions, they are the exceptions rather than the rule. The fact is that most people who work in the real estate industry are not positioning themselves to where the real money is. They simply work to support the development of riches in real estate by others.

All too often I have heard young real estate professionals ponder the disparity between the $25,000 to $30,000 a year they struggle to make, and the multimillions super real estate developers and deal makers like Donald Trump make annually. Certainly there are cases where inherited wealth has made it easier to succeed on this level, but there are also cases of real estate dynamos who come from nothing and position themselves through resourcefulness, hard work, and ingenuity to play in the real estate big leagues. They make large sums of money by learning how to control the game.

For those in the real estate industry who have been curious about what makes real estate dynamos tick, the stories of four successful people illustrate how they got to the lucrative top of the field. David Solomon started out by buying small office buildings and later used his profits to develop his own office complexes, while Bach Realty's Debrah Charaton made her millions in real estate by putting together buyers with their projects. In California, Robert Goodman added a new twist to the real estate game: He learned that there was a great deal of hidden profits to be found in buying public companies in order to develop their undervalued properties. First Realty Reserve's Jeffrey Britz started in the apparel business, then scored big in real estate, and now is pursuing a multitude of other investments. They each had their own methods, all were determined, all succeeded. There are many players in the real estate game, but few succeed to the dimensions of these dynamos. Says Solomon, "I don't believe in losing," a statement that is clear evidence of the tenacity and determination it takes to succeed.

DAVID SOLOMON

DAVID SOLOMON OF SOLOMON EQUITIES

"Sometimes you just have to work through the problems if you want something to happen. Often what separates the winners from the losers is their determination in solving problems."

A dire prediction of David Solomon's confrontation with his first costly mistake appears in an article in *Manhattan, Inc.'s* May 1985 issue on New York's young real estate dynamos, "The Erector Set—Would-be dynasty builders of the second wave."Up to then, the 33-year-old David Solomon had a brilliant, if not flawless, career. After serving a few years teaching at the University of Virginia, the Cornell and Harvard trained architect decided it was time for him to stop teaching and jump into the real estate game himself.

In 1975, Solomon, then 24, bought an empty manufacturing building in Manhattan with just $50,000 down, renovated it, and later sold it for $450,000. This first heartening venture was later followed by a string of successful office building purchases and renovations around Fifth Avenue below 42nd Street. By 1980, his activities had netted him profits in excess of $5 million. Solomon proved his ability in condo conversions with equal expertise when he bought two buildings on East 72nd and East 86th Streets in Manhattan.

With his proven success and experience behind him, Solomon was now ready to play in real estate's big leagues. He had amassed a respectable amount of capital from his previous profits but certainly not enough to build a huge skyscraper on Fifth Avenue. But Solomon did not want to wait; he had big ideas and wanted to apply them at once. He acquired the capital he needed by taking in big corporate partners. For the construction of his 44-story commercial and office building on 49th Street and Fifth Avenue, Tower 49, Solomon joined forces with one of New York's financial powerhouses, First Boston. For Astor Terrace, Solomon's luxurious condominium project on 93rd Street and Second Avenue, Solomon established a joint venture with the Equitable Life Assurance Society.

Both Tower 49 and Astor Terrace were outstanding successes. The recently completed Tower 49, which required over $25 million to construct and develop, is already 100-percent leased at well-above-average midtown prices, and Astor Terrace is planning to sell out all 290 units for close to $105 million on a cost of less than $70 million; 90 percent of the units have already been sold. "But two big hits don't make a third," said the writer in *Manhattan, Inc.*, "The $4,000 per square foot purchase of the Rizzoli and Coty building assemblage could become Solomon's first costly mistake."

"Nonsense," says Solomon. "At the time that the city designated my buildings as landmarks, which for most other people would have meant an end to the construction project, I just became more determined to fight the designation until I won." Adds the ever confident Solomon, "I don't believe in losing."

Solomon's joint acquisition of the Rizzoli and Coty buildings on 56th Street and Fifth Avenue could very well be written as a case study in complex and creative real estate deal-making for MBA students. Solomon's negotiations to acquire one of Manhattan's choicest pieces of real estate were absolutely flawless. However, the political entanglement that followed with the city's Landmark Preservation Commission could easily make for still another great business school case study.

"The Rizzoli thing is a story within itself," says Solomon. "First I was told that I could never assemble the site on that corner of the city. Then, after I did it, the city, egged on by 'anonymous' competition and neighbors, tried to destroy me with a landmark designation." Problems plagued Solomon every step of the way in the Rizzoli project. No matter how shrewdly he was able to solve each one, another just seemed to pop out in front of him. Solomon's wisdom is "Sometimes you just have to work through the problems if you want something to happen. Often what separates the winners from the losers is their determination in solving problems."

Problem number one: assembling the site. The Rizzoli site on the corner of 56th and Fifth Avenue had many different owners and also many different prospective buyers. One owner lived in Italy, another in Germany. Both were initially contacted by Solomon; both did not want to sell. Solomon's solution: "Every few weeks I was in Europe to negotiate. Sometimes I would fly over just for an hour's meeting." Solomon's persistence and brash, confident style won him the respect and admiration of the European owners, who marveled at the aspiration of the young American *wunderkind*. Says Solomon Equities partner Joel Pawe, himself a European: "David has a winning quality. People like him. He simply decided to take the time to get to know the owners and win them over. His dynamism represented what they like about America."

Solomon and his partner, First Boston Corporation, paid an unprecedented $4,000 per square foot for the site. To offset the high land costs, the partnership paid $15.7 million for the unused development rights, known in the real estate industry as "air rights," of the neighboring church, which allowed them to build a taller building on the site than the ordinary zoning for the location would permit. The planned 450,000-square-foot building on the site would then have a land cost of $136 per buildable foot. According to Mr. Travelstead, chairman of First Boston Real Estate, "Before we started I said that if the site costs less than $170 a buildable square foot, the project would work economically."

With the site assembled through successfully negotiated deals with the various overseas and domestic property owners, the air rights purchased, and the financing all put in place, it seemed as if nothing could stop Solomon now from attaining his greatest achievement to date—a beautiful skyscraper constructed on one of Manhattan's choicest sites. But as is all too often the case in deal making, just when you think you have the deal closed, someone or something kicks open the door. In this case it was the city, which attempted to bust open the deal by designating two of the buildings on the site as historic landmarks, which prevented construction, just after Solomon and his partners had finished years of work and $86 million in investments to assemble the site. First Boston's Travelstead screamed that the city was "landmarking by ambush." The project's political problems were even compounded by the very nonpolitical forces working behind the scenes. The old saying that politics makes for odd bedfellows certainly applies here, particularly when there were business as well as political interests at stake. Preservationists, like writer Brendan Gill and the Municipal Art Society's Anthony Wood, who supported the city's landmark designation, found themselves allied and championed by Donald Trump, the owner and developer of the flashy Trump Tower diagonally across from the Rizzoli site.

Travelstead stated in a February 15 *New York Times* article that Trump had wanted earlier to buy the Rizzoli site, or at least be allowed to become a 50 percent partner in the project. When Travelstead refused, Trump reportedly remarked, "I can't imagine a tower going up that would block the view of the people who bought apartments from me—unless, of course, my name were on the project." The *New York Times* further quotes Travelstead quoting Donald Trump: "I hope you don't have any problem with the Municipal Art Society, and I'm telling you I can be of great benefit to seeing that the project goes ahead."

Coincidentally, Mr. Trump was listed as one of the five-member Municipal Art Society's Committee for the Future of Fifth Avenue, which was formed later that year. According to the *New York Times*, Trump "vehemently denied that he wanted a stake in the project." Trump was quoted as stating that his objection to the project was solely on the basis that the building would be detrimental to the "light and air" on Fifth Avenue. *Wall Street Journal* reported Trump saying about the Rizzoli project: "Overall, it's a negative thing. The buildings are true and outstanding landmarks. Besides, it's the only area on that part of Fifth Avenue where there's a great deal of light and air." This was a very odd statement coming from a man who was also reported in the same *Wall Street Journal* article as being widely criticized for demolishing some friezes on the old Bonwit Teller building to make way for the construction of Trump Tower a few years ago.

"In the face of adversity we succeeded through calm patience and persistence," says Solomon. "On January 31, 1985, we were landmarked; between then and April 16, 1986, we had to work through every major city agency to get it approved—any agency turndown would have killed the project."

On April 17, 1986, Solomon won final city approval from the Board of Estimate. The vote was 11 to 0 in favor of the project. Everyone from the mayor, who had two votes on the board, to all the other various city representatives approved the project. Solomon had won their approval by redesigning the building to maintain the original facades of the Rizzoli and Coty buildings and planning to build the planned residence and office building on top of them.

Solomon said that even with all its trouble, the experience of the Rizzoli project was a very valuable one. It reemphasized his belief in the tenets of his personal business philosophy, which he believes are important keys to success, particularly in the complex real estate industry.

"A couple of things are very important," says Solomon. "First of all, patience. Patience to weather the storm; patience to see the storms coming; and when the sailing is clear, to know when the squalls may occur." Adds Solomon, "I think it's important to treat everybody equally and fairly in business—everyone should be given some common courtesy and respect, whether it's the company chairman or the janitor. Anybody in my company who has not followed that rule has not lasted here—that goes for construction crews and bankers. That's how the Rizzoli thing happened. I dealt fairly and listened carefully and asked questions frequently."

Solomon believes that it is important to be able to stand a little distance away; in order to achieve a perspective, you've got to listen to people. "It takes a very complex effort to build buildings today anywhere, but particularly in New York," says Solomon. "There are a lot of flamboyant people out there—but I choose not to be one of them. I'm eccentric in a certain way—I don't follow things too logically. I don't follow things linearly—I don't think business operates that way. I feel there are too many complex things happening—it's almost like a chess game—and that's a quality that I am proud of. To reach a conclusion in any deal you need to see the whole board, not just a few squares."

Solomon is convinced that it is not the money that drives him to succeed, but rather his pride. Pride in oneself involves a continuing fascination with challenging your own abilities and intellectual capabilities by setting your large and small tasks. "I keep telling people that I work hard so I can afford my pleasures. I would like to take time off to work in a few kitchens in Europe. Sailing, cooking, and buying antiques are my major loves. If you always take yourself too seriously and don't make time for hobbies, you'll get an ulcer."

Says Solomon's partner, Joel Pawe, "David always tells me, 'Let's avoid the cabs—let's walk it.' " Pawe says this is another key to Solomon's success: He walks the city constantly, always keeping an eye open for new properties to be acquired and developed. As for the future, Solomon says, "We are doing away with residential and are focusing more on commercial. We are looking at two commercial office buildings. Large chunks of office space will be in demand in the late 1980s and early 1990s, and that's when we plan to be onstream with all our office space. We believe the demand will be there for office space or we wouldn't be doing it, because we have too much to lose." Pawe is confident about Solomon's ability to handle risk, both now and in the future. "David literally put everything on the line to build this firm, he risked everything. It could have gone the other way and he could have been wiped out, but he really believed in himself. That's why he is a winner."

DEBRAH LEE CHARATAN

DEBRAH LEE CHARATAN
OF BACH REALTY

"Whatever we have, we must want." Instead of trying to sell the one listing she had, she asked every caller who responded to her ad what he or she was looking for and said she would find it for them. When she went back to cold calls, she could then tell owners, "I have a buyer. Do you want to sell?"

At age 29, Debrah Lee Charatan is considered one of the 10 most successful women in the United States. She started in the real estate business at 17 as a secretary. In 1980, at the age of 23, she opened Bach Realty Inc. By 1986 Bach Realty had gross sales in excess of $200 million.

More than any other quality, Ms. Charatan's success reflects her work ethic. At the age of 14, she was working a 40-hour week in a bakery in addition to her school work. By 15, the owner of the bakery had put her in charge of the 10 other high school kids who worked there, though most were older than her.

Charatan went to work full time immediately upon graduation from high school. Within a few months she was managing over 10 separate apartment buildings containing over 1,000 units. Simultaneously, she attended college in the evening, graduating with honors.

Charatan decided to open a real estate brokerage firm when she was 23. She borrowed $2,000 and rented an 8-by-10-foot office in the basement of a building in which she now leases an entire floor. Her first and immediate necessity was to find a building owner who wanted to sell and, more important, who would let her handle the deal. She began methodically calling property owners. After three weeks and hundreds of calls, the owner of a 100,000-square-foot loft building finally said yes. She ran a three-line classified ad for the property in the Sunday *New York Times*, and calls began coming in. But instead of trying to sell her one listing, she asked every caller what he or she was looking for and told them that she would find it. When she went back to cold calls she could then tell owners: "I have a buyer, do you want to sell?"

"I can still remember my first deal as if it had happened five minutes ago," she recalls. "It was going to fall through. Everyone was arguing and one of the buyers got fed up, announced that the deal was off, and started to leave the room. I leaped up, physically barred the door with my body, and asked that he give me a chance to try to iron this out." Within the hour all the participants were delighted and the deal was made.

Today, she has over 20 salespeople working for her. Her employees are all women, most of whom make over $100,000 a year. Charatan points out that "women can be excellent workers; they are very cool under pressure and have an amazingly strong desire to succeed."

Charatan takes great pride in the fact that she hires inexperienced people and turns them into $100,000-plus income earners. She looks for people who are "hungry" and want to succeed to the point that they won't take "no" for an answer.

While Debrah Charatan is justifiably proud of her singular business achievement, she is even prouder of her young son, with whom she spends as much time as possible.

Charatan has strong motivation: "Whatever we have, we must want; I just wanted more than most people."

ROBERT GOODMAN

ROBERT GOODMAN OF GOODTAB MANAGEMENT COMPANY

"I am going to take you out on appointments with me and send you out with our top salesman. Don't talk. Listen. Watch the facial expressions and take time to learn about people, because it will be your most valuable lesson in business."

"I always knew someday I would become an independent businessman in real estate," says real estate financier Robert N. Goodman. Even in high school, when his friends spoke of going into medicine and law, Goodman knew his interests were in a field he had been exposed to at a very early age. "My father is a real estate broker and developer, and when I was young we would spend many hours driving around looking at real estate projects."

Goodman attended college at the University of Western Ontario in London, Canada. Although eager to experience college life, he soon tired of academic subjects that had no direct relationship to the real estate business. "I went for one year and dropped out, at the age of 19, in 1972. Finishing my last exam by midafternoon, I packed up my belongings, moved back to Toronto, and went to work the next day as a real estate agent in my father's real estate brokerage firm." Goodman, 33, now president and sole owner of Goodtab Management Company in Beverly Hills, California, has been in real estate ever since that day.

"My father said on my first day at work: 'For the next twelve months I am going to take you out on appointments with me and send you out with our top salesman. Don't talk. Listen. Watch the facial expressions and take time to learn about people, because it will be your most valuable lesson in business." Goodman earned $100 a week for that year and followed his father's advice. "I made $5,000 my first year, and then, at the age of 20, my father told me I was on my own—no salary, just commission. I made $490,000 in commissions that year, netting $245,000, and never looked back."

A few years later Goodman tired of the brokerage business. He did not like being neither a buyer nor a seller and the feeling of having no control over the properties he represented. "Too many deals were falling by the wayside that should have been done," says Goodman. "At the age of 25, I decided to strike out on my own and move to the United States, which had always intrigued me as a more aggressive and challenging market with many real estate opportunities." Goodman and his wife started looking at major cities in the western United States for a place to live. They narrowed their choices down to Denver and Los Angeles and chose L.A.

Goodman settled in Los Angeles and started to buy and develop industrial properties in rapid succession. His timing was good, and he saw property values run up with the rapid inflation of the late 1970s. One of his first areas of concentration was the Irvine Ranch near Newport Beach.

In his first year in Los Angeles, Goodman began to make a lot of money in real estate and also in commodity futures trading. He traded commodities in gold, copper, and British pounds. "At that time gold was trading between $150 to $200 per ounce. It was easy to make money when gold was trading in a narrow range, but when gold started moving $50 a day and ran up from $200 to $800 I got out. Unfortunately, I missed the run up in gold," Goodman pauses, smiles, and takes a deep breath, "but fortunately I missed the collapse in gold as well."

Between commodity futures trading and real estate speculation, Goodman made his first million at the age of 25. "For one year I went through a phase of having success go to my head and thinking that I could do no wrong, and I started losing money in real estate investments." At about that time during 1979, Goodman read an article in *Esquire* magazine, on REITs (Real Estate Investment Trusts). "I had never heard about REITs before; I called the author in New York, and he put me in touch with a fellow in New York who he got most of his information from." That fellow was Ken Campbell, an expert on REITs and author of a newsletter called *Realty Stock Review*. Campbell told Goodman about equity-oriented REITs that were quite profitable and "clean" (not weighted down with bad properties and foreclosures). He pointed out that many of the REITs had stocks that were trading at a fraction of their real property values.

Goodman left Campbell's office with a list of 200 public REITs and decided to stop all his real estate development projects and just study and buy undervalued REITs. Goodman found that by buying controlling interests in depressed stocks in REITs he could buy income-producing properties in major markets in the United States for as low as 30 cents to 40 cents on the dollar. Since 1980 Goodman has concentrated his efforts in buying publicly traded REITs. In 1980 he ran across the Denver Real Estate Investment Association, which traded over the counter and owned about 20 income-producing properties in Denver, including Stouffer's Inn by the airport, the 550,000-square-foot Lakeside mall, two apartment buildings across from the Cherry Creek Country Club, and the 300,000-square-foot office park called Diamond Hill, which lies south of Mile High football stadium.

Goodman went to his bank in Canada to get advice on how to finance the acquisition of this company. He had already quietly accumulated 4 percent of the company at $14 to $16 per share and now needed to look for partners to acquire the whole company. The bank suggested he visit First City Financial Corp., the Belzberg family investment company in Vancouver. Goodman went into a joint venture with the family and in November of 1980 launched a tender offer for 100 percent of the outstanding shares at $37.15 per share. "We were successful in acquiring 82 percent of the shares in the first few weeks, then bought all minority shares 90 days later. Over the next two and one-half years, all of the properties were resold at a very substantial profit."

The acquisition of the Denver Real Estate Investment Association required $42 million in cash plus an assumption of $40 million in fixed-rate mortgages. The acquisition-related debt was borrowed at floating bank rates, which at the time in 1981 were as high as 21 to 22 percent. Even in light of the high financing costs, Goodman was able to make money on the deal. He says that one of the key ingredients to any deal is buying right. "I take a good, long, hard look at the upside potential, but spend 10 times the effort analyzing the downside risks. If you buy right so that in the worst case scenario you will come out whole or with a modest profit, then you can be aggressive." Goodman adds, "When we bought the property [the Denver REIT] the circumstances could not have been worse. The Denver market had peaked and started to collapse; the oil industry turned down; the economy was going into a recession and interest rates were high; but because we bought right, we made money."

In 1982 Goodman was on the warpath again. He started accumulating stock in Wincorp Realty Investments. Wincorp had been in business since 1945 and had previously run harness racing at Hollywood Park Racetrack. It had acquired land in City of Industry, California, to build a new racetrack in anticipation of a move from Hollywood Park. But that move never came, and the land sat idle for 15 years. The Pomona Freeway was built during that time, and one mile of freeway was fronting Wincorp's property. In the early 1970s, Puente Hills Mall was built on the property as a joint venture with the Ernest Hahn Company, and an area over 1.2 million square feet was developed. Wincorp also developed a 125-acre business park adjacent to the mall and developed 620 garden apartments across the street from the mall and still had over 40 acres that remained undeveloped.

"When I got involved in 1982, Wincorp was slowly turning from a harness racing company, in which I had no interest, to a real estate holding company. But the market value of the publicly held securities did not reflect the true value of its real estate assets. One reason was that there was still 40 to 50 acres in the Puente Hills project that were undeveloped and not producing revenues but were clearly worth at least $500,000 an acre." Goodman again began quietly buying shares in Wincorp, which was traded on the American Stock Exchange at between $15 to $17 per share. Goodman ultimately acquired 18 percent of the outstanding shares with a group of investors and became Wincorp's largest shareholder. In the fall of 1983 Goodman requested a seat on its board of directors, which was denied. He then ran a proxy solicitation to be elected to their board, which he won. Goodman remembers, "As soon as I was elected as a director of the company, Lehman Brothers was hired to seek a buyer. By mid-1984, Hollywood Park, Inc. had acquired the harness racing business, and a unit of New England Mutual Life Insurance had agreed to purchase all the real estate assets of Wincorp for a total value of $42 per share." The transaction closed in December of 1984 and made the front page of the *Wall Street Journal* on January 5, 1985.

In late 1984, Goodman started to accumulate shares in CleveTrust Realty Investors, a Cleveland, Ohio-based REIT with assets in Texas, Colorado, and Oklahoma. Goodman currently owns approximately 8.5 percent of its shares and is the largest shareholder in the company. The company is traded over the counter with 2 million shares outstanding. On January 23, 1986, Goodman made a formal offer of $20 per share, in cash, to acquire all the assets of the trust. The management of CleveTrust has not as yet accepted Goodman's offer. Goodman believes that the company will provide value beyond $20 per share after he takes it over as a privately held firm because he can operate it more effectively and will have a greater incentive to reduce vacancy rates and overhead.

Goodman, married and the father of two, believes it is important to develop interests outside one's career so as not to become "a one dimensional person." Goodman's main outside interests are his family and charitable organizations. As for his view of the future, he says, "I feel that the next decade, from the viewpoint of a professional real estate investor, is generally one of optimism. I think that the deregulation in the financial services industry will be a great boom to young entrepreneurs so long as it is not abused."

Goodman's goal is to continue to assemble a "massive" portfolio of high-quality income-producing properties in major urban markets throughout the western United States. He still believes the best way to buy wholesale without assuming the developer's risk is through the purchase of REITs and other publicly traded real estate companies. Goodman intends to continue to focus on a formula that has already proven successful. Once you find a winning formula it pays to be consistent and stay with it.

JEFFREY BRITZ

JEFFREY BRITZ OF FIRST REALTY RESERVE

"As far as I am concerned, the only two meaningful things in life are my love of my family and my love of my work. The money is just for feeling good—it only helps us live well. I don't think money is true security. I think security is in your gut, not your pocket."

Jeffrey Britz has certainly come a long way. "When was the last time you knew a Jewish kid from Brooklyn who met the chief of the Comanches?" says Britz. Britz is referring to one of his most recent outside investments—his financing of the Indian Development Opportunities Corp. (IDOC), which conducts bingo parlors on Indian reservations throughout the western United States. Bingo is approved as a tax-exempt business on Indian reservations and, according to Britz, "is very profitable" as well. Britz particularly enjoys this investment because "it's a chance to make some money while helping a group that has been economically disadvantaged—it makes me feel terrific." But Britz, as we shall see, never does anything on a small scale. His partners in IDOC include the chief auditor of gaming at Harrah's and the chairman of Economic Research Associates.

Britz, 41, is the president and founder of the Manhattan-based First Realty Reserve. In the first three years of its operation, the company has purchased over $250 million worth of properties throughout California, the Carolinas, Florida, Georgia, and Texas. But Britz's entrepreneurial career goes back to when he was 22 and took over his family's ailing garment business. "I entered college—NYU—and spent exactly one day there. I was always more interested in business deals than anything else," recalls Britz. "I probably was trapped into going into the family business because I had to support my mother and sisters."

When Britz took over the family business it was virtually bankrupt. He brought it from $600,000 to $45 million in revenues within the next 10 years. The company, Pacesetter

Industries, started out as a supplier of fabric to tie manufacturers. In the first four years Britz increased sales from $600,000 to $6 million and arranged for a public offering which brought in $400,000 in working capital. Britz then increased his market share and arranged a secondary public offering in 1972, which brought in $4.8 million.

With this capital Britz was able to embark on a series of aggressive acquisitions. In 1972, he acquired the largest necktie manufacturer in the United States, France Neckwear, for $5 million, adding another $20 million in sales to his company. During the following three years, Britz's acquisitions included another neckwear company, a men's pants manufacturer, two belt companies, and a ladies' import company. In addition, he had obtained licenses to produce accessories for the La Coste, Fila, and Bronzini brand names. By the age of 33, Britz had plants throughout the southern United States, offices in the Orient, and over 2,000 employees. Then, in 1983, Victor Kiam, of Remington shaver fame, bought the company and added it to his rapidly growing conglomerate.

Britz recalls that he started First Realty Reserve as a hobby, part-time in 1982. "When I sold Pacesetter—it was towards the end of March in 1983—I think I took the weekend off and then started First Realty Reserve full time in April." What started out as a part-time investment partnership he had set up among friends, developed into a full-scale syndication firm selling equity interest in real estate projects through over 100 securities dealers nationwide. Britz concentrated his real estate investments predominantly in the Sun Belt. Some of the properties that the firm currently owns include Plaza Towers (the first skyscraper in downtown New Orleans); the Wells Fargo Building in downtown Portland; and over 25 shopping centers, office buildings, and apartment complexes throughout the southern and western United States.

Britz has interesting personal and business philosophies, which are often intertwined: "As far as I am concerned the only two meaningful things in life are my love of my family and my love of my work. The money is just for feeling good—it only helps us live well. I don't think money is true security. I think security is in your gut, not your pocket."

Although Britz claims he comes to work to "have a nice time," he does have certain rules about running his business:

1. He has all his employees on some kind of incentive pay that makes up a significant portion of their earnings.
2. He tries to treat people like adults, and leave them alone to do their jobs.
3. He concentrates on what people do right rather than on what they do wrong, because people perform better if they feel good about themselves.
4. He believes that if you hire the wrong people you will screw up the first three principles, so you'd better hire the right people.

Britz claims that because it's very hard to hire good people, it's important to hang on to them when you find them, and you do this by treating them as you would like them to treat you. "Your business ethics should not be any different than your personal ethics," states Britz. He finds the only reason that people maintain a dual set of ethics is because money is such a tremendous temptation. "Money should never be your god."

Part of Britz's philosophy is based on knowing yourself—understanding who you are and what you do well. "I think the most important thing is that you keep a sense of humility and you don't become imbued with self-importance. I very much prefer getting things going and leaving others to run them. I am not a manager, I like the deal aspects of business. I do not want to be an investment banker, I'd rather not do deals for others, just for myself and my associates."

Britz adds, "I believe you should work hard, but I also believe you should get away—fairly frequently—which I do not do often enough. When I do, I feel much better, and perform very well."

Britz admits that there's a lot of pressure in being a business owner, but he does not believe entrepreneurs should kid themselves by claiming they work hard for their family. "That's bull. You should work hard because you want to." On the day of our interview, Britz woke at four-thirty A.M., ran, showered and dressed. At six-fifteen he listened to his daughter play the piano, arrived at work at seven, and was in his dynamo interview at eight. Britz did not return home before seven that evening, but his return was probably preceded by a brief workout in the company's Universal gym weight room. He may have encountered another First Realty Reserve employee there—Art Shamsky, a former star of the New York Mets baseball team.

In the face of the new tax laws, Britz admits that the real estate investment equation is changing. With Congress limiting tax advantages on real estate investments, deals will have to be based more on economic benefits (appreciation and profit) than on tax savings. In search of better returns and lower prices, Britz has turned his attention to reviewing foreclosure properties. But still, since much of the real estate syndications in his company, as well as in the industry in general, heavily weigh the tax benefits, he has implemented plans to change his deal structuring and syndication techniques so they are still appealing under the new tax law.

But should the tax laws slightly slow down his real estate business the ever-resilient Britz would then probably turn to another one of his part-time ventures and develop *it* into a full-time industry. He has already invested in a few high tech companies, and his most recent hobby was financing the company that was acquiring the franchise rights to the Aca Joe clothing stores throughout the Sun Belt states and Asia. He and his associates have already invested $1 million and are in the process of completing a public offering. Britz's partner in the venture and the head of the company is the ex-president of Casual Corner and head of U.S. operations for Murjani, the company Gloria Vanderbilt is associated with. They have retained Marc McCormick International to negotiate a joint venture with a Japanese retailer to establish Aca Joe stores throughout Asia. But if this and all his other projects should ever bore him, Britz can always join his friend, the chief of the Comanches, in working full time to build a gaming operation that would no doubt rival Bally, Resorts International, and Caesar's Palace combined.

LEVERAGE YOUR TIME AND MONEY AS WELL AS YOUR COMPANY

There is a lot of talk filling cheap newspapers and magazines, as well as cable TV stations, about getting rich using leverage. That is using other peoples' money or a bank's money, typically highly levered loans, to acquire an asset—most often real estate. Most often, the advice that you receive amounts to nothing more than hot air. Most of the self-made gurus and millionaires made their money not in real estate, but in selling you and me, and thousands of others, their series of special tapes, manuals, and seminars for $395 on "How to get rich in real estate."

Often this literature and these seminars sing of the wonders of leverage, describing schemes involving the purchase of real estate with "nothing down." Although in fact it *is* possible to purchase real estate for nothing down, all too often you get what you pay for. The courses merely show you how to creatively assume someone else's problem. Often these assumptions require precariously high debt assumptions, frequently with big balloon payments that come due before the

171

budding young real estate baron can either negotiate practical refinancing or afford it. One thing that the gurus forget to tell you is that balloon payments are like neutron bombs; they kill all the people involved but leave the building still standing. Most of the people involved in attending these seminars are neither educated nor sophisticated enough to implement these "tools for success" properly. They would do better by keeping their hard-earned $395 in a savings account for retirement. Not everyone is cut out to be rich or an entrepreneur. I must admit that there are some motivational and training tapes and seminars that are very beneficial. My caution here, however, is directed against those programs that abuse the public by advocating get rich quick schemes that promote the use of imprudent financial strategies and unreasonable financial risk. When inexperienced people take these sorts of risks, they often have a greater chance of losing what little they have than making a large fortune.

So what then is all this talk about leverage? What is leverage and how can those of us who are savvy use it practically to achieve wealth? First, leverage is defined as the process by which we use a smaller force to control a much larger force. In construction a laborer would use a crow bar to pry open a heavy door or a hand truck to lift many times his weight. In business, financiers and entrepreneurs employ leverage to control or acquire a valuable asset with an investment of capital many times smaller than the asset. They can do this in acquiring real estate by using bank loans or raising money from investors, or in acquiring a corporation, through the use of loans and floating public offerings.

The key in using leverage to acquire wealth is first to find an opportunity. It is not so important whether the opportunity is one in business, real estate, or technology. What matters is that it be undervalued or have the potential to create greater value than its original cost or investment requirement. Particularly in real estate and business acquisition opportunities, finding an asset that is undervalued and for which you can negotiate a purchase below market is one of the first steps to set up a healthy situation for using leverage. The process that follows, which allows you to acquire an asset for a small percentage of the sale price or to take a percentage share of the opportunity for finding and structuring the opportunity, involves obtaining loans from the bank that are lent against the value of the asset and/or selling equity interest to other investors at a price higher than the cost of your own acquisition.

Often you will want to "tie up" the opportunity through a purchase contract or option to buy before showing it to banks or outside investors. Understanding the true value of the asset and how it relates to the values of the current market requires experience, research, and hard work. If you find a good project and do your homework to ensure that it has value, you then can take the next step to apply leverage.

Just as David Solomon has proved the value of practical leverage in achieving wealth in real estate, the examples that follow, on dynamos Jay Jordan and John Cade, provide fine examples of the way to create wealth by using leverage to acquire companies. All these entrepreneurs, however, are savvy, sophisticated investors. Their experience wasn't acquired overnight, and certainly not through a $395 training course. They earned their success through years of hard work, developing expertise in understanding their business and the market. Instead of trying to take on large projects on their own immediately, which would require financial commitments over their heads, they started small and often took in financial partners in larger projects. They met their challenges and survived their setbacks along the way because they learned how to control their growth and spread their risk.

The ability to understand and manage risk is probably one of the key elements in an entrepreneur's success, if not in his or her very survival. Maturity and patience are probably the most important personal characteristics in managing risk. Jay Jordan points out that a sense of perspective is important to develop an understanding of both your business and personal life. As David Solomon said earlier, "You have to be able to see the whole chessboard, not just a few squares."

Like most sharp instruments or tools we use, leverage is a double-edged sword; it can cut both ways. The same method we use to maximize the speed and ability with which we acquire wealth can bury us with the same speed if we don't cover our risks and anticipate possible losses. Failure is to be expected. Stocks and property values go down as well as up. Prepare yourself for adverse changes in the market, in addition to your own human errors, and you will be a survivor rather than a victim. The ability of an entrepreneur to keep his or her mistakes from being fatal is what allows him or her to stay in the game long enough to find a winning hand.

Jordan and Cade both experienced failure early. In each case the dynamo found it to be the best preparation for their future success. They used leverage both through bank loans and through public financing to build their empires. They each had great dreams and a dedicated plan to achieve their goals. They managed their risks, worked hard, and persisted until they achieved those goals. One is continuing to expand his empire, the other's plans were cut short by a tragic death. As Jordan points out, no other catastrophe in business can compare to a loss of life. Keeping both risks, as well as life, in perspective allows us not only to increase our chances of success, but happiness as well.

JAY JORDAN

JAY JORDAN OF THE JORDAN COMPANY

"You get the biggest bang for your buck in buying and owning businesses because you can't capitalize your gains in real estate in a public market like you can for operating companies."

"The only thing that really separates all of us from the skid row drug addict is the luck of the draw—as long as you keep this in mind, you will be better at whatever you do," says John ("Jay") Jordan, 38. Jordan is managing partner of the Jordan Company, which owns controlling interests in over 25 companies with aggregate sales in excess of $1.5 billion. Jay Jordan is a man who likes to keep things in perspective. He is very open and frank about his views on the creation of wealth and risk, and those views are an important part of both his business and his personal philosophy.

At 26, Jordan joined the firm of Carl Marks and Co., Inc., an old line, highly respected, foreign securities firm. At the time Jordan joined Carl Marks, its investment group was primarily involved in venture capital investments and real estate transactions. After having worked on the venture capital side of the business for two years, Jordan decided to develop his own niche within the firm. "I thought the risks in venture capital were greater than the commensurate returns, and I thought I could create a disproportionate rate of return ratio in leverage buy-outs (LBO). At a time when the spectre of hyperinflation was beginning to surface (in the 1970s), I thought the best hedge against inflation was buying and owning operating assets generating growing cash flow. It also appeared that one could achieve substantial returns given minimal levels of risk by acquiring historically successful companies. I, therefore, made the decision to enter the burgeoning leverage buy-out industry," says Jordan. Jordan spent the next eight years at Carl Marks focusing on acquiring companies on a leveraged basis for his own and the Carl Marks partners' personal portfolio.

The objective was to receive a vastly superior rate of return given the level of risk without the responsibility of day-to-day management. He looked for old line, historically profitable companies with proven experienced management teams and a proprietary product or market niche. The idea was to employ leverage in acquiring the companies to enhance the rate of return on the equity investment. In order to responsibly assume the financial risk of leverage, it became essential to select the right companies, ones that offered very little business risk.

Jay was convinced that the leveraged acquisition of businesses provided an even greater return than leveraged purchases of real estate. Says Jordan, "You get the biggest bang for your buck in buying and owning businesses because you can't capitalize your gains in real estate in a public market like you can for operating companies." Jordan would capitalize on acquisition opportunities by buying businesses with a small equity investment and having the banks provide the rest of the capital required for the purchase through loans made against the company's assets and cash flow. Jordan, therefore, is able to "leverage" his investment by controlling a large asset with a small equity. Says Jordan, "In LBOs, you create wealth by imposing on these companies the risk of leverage while you personally stand to gain from its profitability."

Initially, Jordan found the equity capital required for his deals by syndicating the acquisition with a number of financial institutions. As he made more money personally, he syndicated less and used more of the firms' money so he could control a bigger share of the acquired firm. Now Jordan does not syndicate his deals at all; he acquires them 100 percent for the Jordan Company's account.

Having spent eight successful years at Carl Marks, Jordan left the firm with another individual whom he had brought in by the name of David W. Zalaznick and formed The Jordan Company for the purpose of continuing the leverage buyout activity that Jordan had initiated and pursued at Carl Marks.

Jordan's current buy-out "niche" is the acquisition of "middle market firms" in the private sector with purchase prices between $10 to $100 million. He gives two reasons for buying mid-sized private companies.

1. The private market is much less efficient than the public market in terms of valuation. There is not an efficient market for mid-sized private companies especially in towns like Salina, Kansas; Red Oak, Iowa, and the like. The large New York investment banking firms are not very active in these areas, which lessens competitive bidding. Often Jordan will find his deals through smaller regional brokerage firms and be able to acquire these companies at 20 to 40 percent discounts to what the same company would be valued if trading in the public marketplace. Often Jordan later profits by selling the companies that he buys through large New York investment banking firms. Lehman Brothers is currently selling two companies; Lazard is selling one; and Drexel is financing one other.

2. Acquiring companies for between $10 to $100 million justifies the time and effort Jordan puts in in structuring the acquisition in terms of the size of the transaction, at the same time, the transactions are small enough that he can afford to acquire the companies for the Jordan Company's own account without the need for outside equity. Jordan also points out that acquiring companies of this size allows him to complete a number of transactions a year, which he wouldn't be able to do if he acquired just one big company. Jordan maintains that "diversification is one of the first principles in our investment philosophy. If we stepped up to half-billion-dollar deals, we would have to either participate in fewer opportunities or take on partners—neither of which we look upon with favor."

The Jordan Company typically buys four companies a year, on average, and sells an equal number a year through either

an outright sale to another investment group, a public company, or by taking the company public.
Jordan's current holdings include:

- *Martin Theatres, Inc.* of Columbus, Georgia, an owner and operator of 420 movie screens in theaters located in Virginia, North Carolina, South Carolina, Kentucky, Tennessee, Georgia, Texas, Alabama, and Florida. Annual sales are approximately $80 million.

- *Bench Craft, Inc.* of Blue Mountain, Mississippi, manufacturer of upholstered furniture sold through independent furniture stores and retail chains. Annual sales are approximately $65 million.

- *Piece Goods Shops Company* of Winston-Salem, North Carolina, the largest privately owned retail fabric chain in the United States, operating over 100 stores in the Southeast, Ohio, and Massachusetts. Annual sales are approximately $70 million.

- *Cape Craftsmen, Inc.* of Elizabethtown, North Carolina, the largest manufacturer and retailer of American decorative items including wood, ceramic, brass, and candle products. Operates 50 retail stores throughout the United States. Annual sales are approximately $50 million.

- *Industrial Sales Co. Inc.* of Baltimore, Maryland, manufacturer and distributor of marine and industrial wire rope, cable, and related products for use in construction, manufacturing, and the maritime trade. Annual sales are approximately $20 million.

- *Leucadia National Corporation* (formerly Talcott National Corporation) of New York, New York, a New York Stock Exchange financial services company primarily engaged in the consumer financial business. The company also has a substantial real estate portfolio and insurance subsidiaries. Total assets are approximately $500 million.

- *Arnold Graphic Industries* of Akron, Ohio, a manufacturer and distributor of business forms, including continuous data processing forms, snap-out forms, and other related products sold to the U.S. Department of Defense. Annual sales are approximately $20 million.

- *Parsons Precision Products, Inc.* of Parsons, Kansas, a manufacturer of large precision fabricated assemblies, high-volume small assemblies and precision machine parts for the U.S. Government, aerospace, and general industry. Annual sales are approximately $15 million.

- *Jones Manufacturing Company* of Birmingham, Alabama, a manufacturer and distributor of plumbing items including products made of cast iron, rubber, plastic, brass, and stainless steel. Annual sales are approximately $35 million.

- *Cal-Style Furniture Manufacturing Company* of Compton, California, manufacturer and distributor of casual dining furniture to mass merchandisers, department stores, specialty furniture shops and furniture showrooms throughout the United States. Annual sales are approximately $40 million.

- *Coronet Manufacturing Company* of Gardena, California, manufacturer of decorative table lamps, floor lamps, and lighting fixtures that are distributed to major retail chains and department stores throughout the United States. Annual sales are approximately $20 million.

- *Sate-Lite Manufacturing Company* of Niles, Illinois, manufacturer of reflector kits and accessories for the bicycle and automotive industries. Annual sales are approximately $15 million.

- *Dura-Line Corporation* of Middlesboro, Kentucky, extrudes plastic pipe for use in drinking water, drainage, and irrigation systems as well as for protective conduit of optical fibre materials. Annual sales are approximately $10 million.

- *Dize Company* of Winston-Salem, North Carolina, maintains three autonomous operating divisions that manufacture and distribute venetian blinds, canvas, and vinyl coverings for items requiring protection from the environment, and awnings and tents for private homes, commercial buildings, etc. Annual sales are approximately $10 million.

- *Eastern Home Products* of Elkhart, Indiana, designer, manufacturer, and marketer of sheet sets, comforters, and mattress pads for waterbeds sold to large mass merchandising chains and department stores. In addition, the company also distributes waterbed accessories such as water treatment kits, patch repair kits, and drain and fill kits. Annual sales of the company are approximately $25 million.

- *Imperial Electric Company* of Akron, Ohio, manufacturer of motor generators and drives that are principally used in the elevator, floor care, and machine tools industries. Annual sales are approximately $25 million.

- *House of Ronnie, Inc.* of New York, New York, manufacturer and distributor of popular-priced sportswear, nightwear, and undergarments for women and girls sold through major chain and department stores. Annual sales are approximately $85 million.

- *OPC Holdings, Inc.*, Universal Paper Goods Company, Inc., Master Products Manufacturing Co., Inc., of Los Angeles, California, manufacturer and distributor of paper filing systems, including file folders, jackets, fasteners, and expandable envelopes. The Master Products division makes metal filing cabinets, paper punches, leather sales cases, and other specialty items. Annual sales are approximately $40 million.

- *The Thomas D. Murphy Company* of Red Oak, Iowa, the largest privately owned calendar and specialty advertising company. Annual sales are approximately $20 million.

- *George Hantscho Company* of Mount Vernon, New York, manufacturer of lithographic offset web printing press systems used for high-volume printing. Hantscho designs its proprietary printing systems, which include advanced accessories such as Colorset and Microink. Annual sales are approximately $40 million.

- *Marisa Christina, Inc.* of New York, New York. Designs, contracts for the manufacture of, and markets an extensive line of women's sweaters under the Marisa Christina trademark. Marisa Christina sweaters are sold through fine department stores and specialty shops. Annual sales are approximately $30 million.

- *Madera Pacific, Inc.* of Rapid City, South Dakota, a manufacturer and distributor (wholesale and retail) of building material products. The company also operates a trucking company, Dakota Pacific Transport, which carries both the company's and outside accounts. Annual sales are approximately $20 million.

It can never be repeated too often when talking about Jordan that perspective, a clear sense of perspective, is a very important component in guiding Jordan's business and personal life. Jordan is particularly keen on his perspective of risk and failure. "When I started, I risked everything because I had nothing to lose. Now that I have money, I don't risk it all; I don't bet the ranch—I have structured my business not to risk anything on one throw of the dice." Jordan sets up each acquisition as an independent entity, the liabilities are born by each business acquisition as a stand-alone enterprise. If something goes wrong, he only loses his investment in that one company. The rest of his holdings remain intact.

But according to Jordan, there are some entrepreneurs who possess a "wildcatter mentality." These are people who will continue to risk everything they've got on the next big deal. For decades the front pages of our business tabloids have continued to chronicle the rise and fall of empire builders whose crash to earth came as fast as their meteoric rise all because they could not grow personally or evolve as their fortunes grew. Like gamblers, they are seduced by the action, the excitement of always having all their chips on the table. "It's silly," says Jordan. "When you begin to take nature for granted, you will get killed. We all operate in a framework of certain natural laws, which we have to understand. If we don't, that's when we get clobbered. The market is very unforgiving."

The paramount of these natural laws, and the one that most reflects personal philosophy, is the ability both to learn from and to anticipate failure. "True long-term entrepreneurs are not blind gamblers. They are just very good at evaluating and managing risk," says Jordan. "The best thing that can ever happen to an entrepreneur is to have a failure of relative magnitude at an early stage of life." When an entrepreneur experiences failure early on, future mistakes will not be as costly. Early failure is the best education that prepares one for the realization that future mistakes are to be anticipated, expected, and planned for.

"When Wall Street collapsed in 1973–1974, a lot of young partners lost everything because they never experienced failure early. They made millions early in their career in the go-go years and never saw the market tank. When they finally saw the other side of the market, they weren't prepared." Jordan had his own 1929 at a young age. "I lost $20,000 in the stock market when I was 21. It may not seem like a lot of money now, but back then, to me it was like the national debt. That's when I learned that things go down as well as up. It was a great experience."

Jordan maintains that an early failure may be humiliating, but for determined entrepreneurs, it serves to strengthen as well as educate. Anticipating and covering your downside risk is very important in business, particularly your own. You can experience losses as long as you don't completely run out of cash—because once you run out of cash, they take you out of the game. The key is staying at the table so you will be able to maintain your position and play out your hand when the right opportunity comes along. If you allow your first failure to be devastating, you won't be around to participate in the second opportunity, which may be a success.

"We have had failures. I have had companies that I have bought that didn't work out. We have had our share of problems, but we are still here," says Jordan. "It's highly unlikely that I will ever go broke other than in a macroeconomic catastrophe because I have structured my business and covered by downside risk to anticipate failure. We even have a company now that is in Chapter 11, but I don't look at it as a catastrophe. I look at it as an opportunity. In business there is no such thing as catastrophe; there is only a temporary interruption of your growth path, only the loss of a life is a real catostrophe." It's important to have a sense of perspective, "business problems can be dealt with successfully."

According to Jordan, personal growth as well as business development is an evolutionary process. "This whole business of being in business is just sort of a game. At some point, you start out with a very distorted and myopic view of the world, and the basic objective is the singular accumulation of wealth. As you begin to accumulate wealth, your targets and objectives begin to change and the amounts do as well. Your targets change, your objectives change, and your overall view of life itself changes. After financial success is achieved, you look for other benchmarks. You want to grow and make even more money for ego purposes, not because you need more money. Money becomes secondary—not a tool any more, just a yardstick to measure your success. If your target is $1 million by 30, then it will be $100 million by 40, and a billion by 50."

Jordan believes that achievement and independence were his major motivation to go into business for himself. "One of the best ways to be truly independent," he says, "is to be financially independent." Jordan believes there is a deep-ridden competitive factor that spurs on entrepreneurs in business, but in their social lives, they are actually very philanthropic and altruistic. Knowing that he had made it on his own is also very important to Jordan. "One of the things I am thankful for is that I did not inherit my career and I never will be tormented by the question of whether or not I truly made it on my own. There are many very successful second-generation entrepreneurs who continually hear their colleagues disparage their accomplishments because of their inheritance. That is a problem I will never have."

So if Jordan has accomplished $2 billion before 40, in sales at least, what could be next before he hits 50? Investment trusts, mutual funds, venture capital, and real estate. Jordan is now in the process of capitalizing on his past reputation of success by floating a two-tiered investment trust on the London stock exchange. He has also set up a money management firm with an eye on acquiring a mutual fund. His money management firm's initial efforts have succeeded in placing $300 million under management, and it plans to have $1.5 to $2 billion within five years. Jordan is also considering a family of public mutual funds including a venture capital fund, and his new real estate group is already up and running. "We are really developing into a full-fledged investment banking firm," says Jordan. But perhaps a more proper term is "merchant banking" because they act as principals in everything they do.

But all bold plans, at least ones that succeed, have some important underlying philosophical tenets behind them. Says Jordan, "Business in general is really not that exotic—people tend to overglamorize it. Basically, it's fundamentals and common sense."

JOHN CADE

JOHN CADE OF CADE INDUSTRIES/EDAC TECHNOLOGIES

How does a marginally profitable firm still in its start-up phase acquire highly profitable companies? Cade knew only two things: he wanted Auto-Air and Advanced Systems Technologies, and he was going to figure out how to get them.

When John Cade came to Denver, Colorado in 1982 it was in search of capital to continue and expand the modest company he had started in the small town of Marinette, Wisconsin. His hope was that his Cade Industries would one day become a major aerospace, electronics, and defense company.

John Cade had had one failure. After several years as a CPA with Touche Ross, a Big Eight accounting firm, and as vice president of sales and marketing with L.E. Jones Company he entered the world of entrepreneurial independence, establishing Cade Manufacturing as a machine shop to service the needs of local industry. The attempt, however, was not successful, and the company went into bankruptcy. Undaunted, Cade raised money from private investors to repurchase the assets of Cade Manufacturing from the bank and he reestablished the company as Cade Industries in 1980. "Aerospace is where the future lies," said Cade, and he founded Cade Industries as an aerospace components manufacturer.

The aerospace industry is one in which it takes time and capital to become a significant player. John Cade was short on both. In need of both working capital and capital for expansion, Cade's first venture into raising money in the public markets almost lost him his company for the second time. His effort ended as an aborted public offering—one in which a company absorbs the legal, accounting, printing, and investment banking expense incurred in preparing a public offering, only to have the deal fall through. It frequently happens through underwriter mismanagement, overvaluing a security, or the closing of a public market window. Whatever the reason, it happened to Cade in his first attempt, and it cost him over $100,000.

Frustrated but far from beaten, Cade regrouped and thought through his strategy for the future. Meanwhile, his company continued to crawl along taking in annual revenues of $500,000. It was clear that in order to make the acquisitions that would allow Cade Industries to grow, Cade would need capital. But how does a marginally profitable firm still in its start-up phase acquire highly profitable companies? Cade wanted Auto-Air Industries of Lansing, Michigan, and Advanced Systems Technologies of Denver, Colorado. The banks were willing to lend money but not enough. Friends and investors had provided financial assistance in the past but were hardly capable of providing it to the tune of the $5.6 million Cade's dream required. Cade knew only two things: he wanted those companies, and he was going to figure out how to get them.

John Cade had a vehicle company through which he could make acquisitions. He had come up with a viable target. Now all he needed was the capital. How was he to find it? He saw the answer in Denver's "penny stock market."

Denver is referred to nationally as the "penny stock" capital of the United States. The title was earned over the years as a result of the western United States' willingness to fund speculative oil and gas and mining companies through low-priced public stock offerings. The compliment of being the capital is a backhanded one; many of the speculative funding in Denver's past led to great hopes but little in the way of revenue, much less earnings. But by 1983 the Denver market had matured to the point where it could orchestrate financings of up to $5 million and had become more diverse, with a broad mix of technology companies. The market, however, was still a place where new ideas could be financed. John Cade had a new idea.

Frequently companies make acquisitions through using excessive debt. Assuming they have the financial strength to do so, they are often in a precarious position when it comes to servicing the debt. John Cade's $500,000 company did not have the borrowing strength alone, so a pure leverage buyout couldn't work. In need of equity financing, Cade went to Denver.

Instead of taking Cade Industries public as a $500,000 company in need of expansion capital, Cade proposed to take Cade Industries public as a company with an option to acquire the profitable private company Auto-Air. By raising public equity capital and exercising the option, public shareholders would own a piece of an aerospace subcontractor whose corporate objective was to grow through acquisition and internal expansion.

The Cade Industries financing turned out to be one the Denver market hadn't seen before. It was priced at 50 cents a share. Was this an early-stage company or a mature one? Auto-Air had been operating for 28 years. There were actually both revenues and profits on a pro-forma basis as the deal was able to disclose fully the activities of Auto-Air.

The Denver market, used to funding concepts prior to their taking shape, grappled with the man from Marinette, Wisconsin, who wanted to build a major aerospace subcontractor. On January 31, 1984, the public deal closed. On January 31, 1984, Cade Industries acquired Auto-Air and soon followed with the acquisition of Advanced Systems Technologies. John Cade, then 35 years old, was the chairman, president, and CEO of a company that at the end of 1984 would show $9.5 million in revenues for the year. Quite a jump from the past year's sales of $500,000!

In January of 1985, the company received its first major engineering contract with Martin Marietta valued at approximately $3.5 million. It was to provide computer performance engineering support to Martin Marietta's Air Traffic Control division in Washington, D.C.

In his 1984 annual report, John Cade wrote, "Of our future . . . while we made considerable progress in 1984 toward achieving our goal of creating a diversified technology company, I am optimistic that 1985 will prove to be even more successful. . . . In 1984 we demonstrated we have the ability to make things happen. In 1985, through acquisition and internal growth, we intend to establish a true 'core.' 1986 will be a period of consolidation for even greater growth and prosperity in 1987."

In 1985 John Cade fulfilled his prophesy. Working alongside the investment banking firms of Kingstone Prato and James J. Duane, Cade more than quadrupled his company's revenues by arranging for another public leveraged buy-out of a $41-million auto and aerospace design engineering company, Gros-ite Industries. Cade acquired Gros-ite, which netted $1.8 million on $41 million in sales in 1985, for $9.9 million. To make this acquisition, Cade set up a shell company called EDAC Technologies, Inc. (EDAC is Cade spelled backwards.) Cade raised $3 million from private investors and funds acquired from Cade Industries, and $5.4 million was provided by a public offering of EDAC stock raised at $5.50 per unit, consisting of a common share of EDAC plus a three-year warrant to purchase Cade stock for $1.87 (Cade was trading at $0.56 at the time of offering). The remaining $1.5 million was provided by a $500,000 bank loan and $1 million in Cade Industry stock.

The acquisition was an amazing feat; it represented a minnow swallowing a whale. The advantage of acquiring this company through the use of a separate public offering that funded the buy-out was that it eliminated a burdensome debt load that would have been provided by a classic leveraged buy-out. Another advantage was that it prevented the further dilution of Cade stock, which would have been substantial if Cade Industries had to file a secondary public offering by itself or $9.9 million. Cade, who owned 32 percent of Cade Industries' stock, made a major effort to grow while maintaining his equity position in the company. The Cade warrants provided in the EDAC stock offering package provided the public with a very interesting and creative additional incentive to buy the new issue. If the warrants are exercised, they will provide Cade Industries with an additional $1.9 million to fund future acquisitions.

At 37, Cade was chairman and CEO of a conglomerate whose combined sales were in excess of $50 million. He had succeeded in fulfilling his promises to his shareholders for 1985 and was well on his way to fulfilling his visions of continued growth for 1986 when his life was cut short by an airplane accident.

Had John lived longer, he would have undoubtedly built an aerospace empire that would have rivaled the conglomerates of Rockwell, Lockheed, and General Dynamics. John Cade was a true dynamo who will be sorely missed by all who knew him.

ON TURNAROUNDS AND RESCUE MISSIONS— ENTREPRENEURS WHO STUMBLED BUT DID NOT FALL

Experience sometimes requires that we make our own mistakes, but wisdom allows us to learn from the mistakes of others. Sometimes entrepreneurs run into trouble. Often it may not be a lack of success that leads them to trouble but rather the uncontrolled rapid growth that may come as a by-product of success.

The never-ending chant of advice from most management consultants and start-up experts, "watch your overhead" and "don't over-expand," is often heeded by entrepreneurs who finance their companies out of their own pockets. Sometimes, though, the temptation to indulge oneself is too great. A large sum of money deposited in the corporate treasury from the proceeds of a public offering or private investment can

195

be very seductive. Entrepreneurs sometimes lose sight of the fact that no amount of money ever amounts to a bottomless well.

In a previous book I devoted a section to partnerships and exhorted the reader to get partnership agreements in writing! But like all legal agreements, the strength of the document is often only as strong as the strength of the cosigner's goodwill and intentions. As the song goes, "Breaking up is hard to do." There are some words to that song that still remain to be written—for instance, "breaking up" for many partnerships may be nothing short of disastrous.

In the stories to follow you will learn how one entrepreneur, Doug Wilson, overcame his corporate excesses before the excesses overcame the company, and how another, Joshua Beren, saw both his partnership and company destroyed only to reemerge and form another more successful and dynamic enterprise.

Also profiled is the unique story of a dynamo, Ted Leonsis, who built and sold a successful publishing enterprise, only to see it falter in the hands of new management. His efforts to repurchase and rebuild his company provides us with yet another example of how often what may be a crisis for one person presents a turnaround opportunity for another.

DOUG WILSON

DOUG WILSON OF DOUG WILSON STUDIOS

"Crisis situations provide the best opportunity; the people who believed in us, who kept buying the stock as it fell, have now made nice profits on their investment. As for the company, it is a lot stronger because the crisis forced us to clean up our act."

On August 15, 1985, there was a huge party in La Jolla, California. The partygoers were celebrating the successful closing of the initial public offering of Doug Wilson Studios, Inc. The check for $1 million was paraded around the room while dozens of champagne bottles were uncorked. Kidder, Peabody's San Diego super stockbroker, Cynthia Ekberg, one of the initial investors in the company, described the party as a "fabulous occasion."

For Doug Wilson, the 42-year-old company chairman and president, the party represented the culmination of over 20 years of hard work, designing, writing, marketing, and creating trends in giftwear, specialty items, and apparel. Prior to 1976, when Wilson first formally established his company to market his designs and products, he was a successful freelance writer and designer. Wilson worked on ad campaigns and TV commercials. He also designed pop-art candles and pub mirrors; commodity products with licensed trademarks such as Hersheys, Lifesavers, and Crayolas; leather sneakers for Keds; and a "Hot-Lips" line of greeting cards; as well as checkbook covers, make-up cases, eyeglasses, bathsheets and ready-to-wear tops for Bloomingdale's, and sheets and pillowcases for Burlington Mills. In 1976, he went into partnership with a large ceramic mug manufacturer to organize "Doug Wilson Designs," which sold over 1 million coffee mugs with catchy phrases and graphics. In 1980, Wilson formed another partnership, which marketed a line of pillowcases, laundry bags, T-shirts, and other novelty items. In 1982, Wilson created a third partnership to develop and market nationally, a line of junior sleepwear, T-shirts, and sportswear through department stores and specialty shops.

Wilson's bright humor and creative designs won him a great deal of attention and acclaim, particularly among a group of local investors (including Ms. Ekberg) who were convinced that Wilson had the potential to be the next Ralph Lauren, Liz Claiborne, or Esprit. Ekberg's client list includes Madonna, Jerry Tsai (President of American Can Corporation), Roy Disney, and another investor, Ian Gardner-Smith, the former founder and chairman of Great American Resources, a publicly held San Diego-based oil and gas company, which manages over $100 million in properties. Ekberg convinced Wilson that in order for him to become an organized marketing organization that could attract the investment capital needed to fund his future growth he needed to consolidate his loosely formed collection of private partnerships into one corporation and bring on a corporate sales and management staff to aggressively promote his designs. Leon Rosenberg, the executive vice president and director of sales and marketing for the famous fashion powerhouse, Esprit, agreed with Ekberg and Gardner-Smith. Rosenberg became an investor and later served as a board member of Doug Wilson Studios, Inc.

Wilson accepted both their advice and capital. By mid-1984, Doug Wilson combined his individual partnerships to form Doug Wilson Studios, Inc. to sell and distribute the full range of Doug Wilson designs and creations and to include a new sportswear line that was being planned on dozens of Wilson's sketch pads. Wilson brought on managers from J.C. Penney and other companies. The new company prospered. Sales grew to over $2.5 million in the first year of operation, and its client list expanded to include Bloomingdale's, Burdines, Dillards, Bambergers, Nordstrom, Abraham & Strauss, Hess Department Stores, May D & F, Dayton's, Ivey's, Jordan Marsh, Macy's, and under a separate label, J.C. Penney, Sears, and Wards to name a few. But growth capital was tight; the company was able to raise another round of private investment capital, but it was not enough to jump into the huge sportswear market, which represented the company's greatest growth potential.

While vacationing in San Diego, investment banker, Steve Prato met Ian Gardner-Smith and Ekberg and soon found himself in Doug Wilson's La Jolla office, excited with hundreds of product samples and sketchpad designs. Prato was overwhelmed, and Kingstone Prato, Inc. was soon to underwrite Doug Wilson Studios initial public offering for $1.2 million. The events that followed the public offering and subsequent celebration were far from "fabulous"; they were more like "disastrous."

The resulting excesses that almost led to Doug Wilson Studios' permanent demise were almost textbook examples of what can happen when entrepreneurs receive a lot of money or success quickly and temporarily stop worrying about "keeping their eyes on the road ahead." In Wilson's case, he allowed others with no common understanding of the ultimate goals to guide the company he created. Overhead and expenses skyrocketed. The new managers and executives lavished themselves with large expense accounts. While on sales trips, they stopped staying at budget hotels or the homes of friends and instead booked into five-star accommodations. Individual hours were shortened and support staff was increased, except in the case of Doug, who continued working off his good old drawing board at his home around the clock. Now two to three people were doing the job previously handled by one, and additional office space had to be rented to house the new support staff. Although the company enhanced and expanded its New York and Los Angeles sales offices, which was a positive step, it also opened a retail store in a posh and expensive San Diego mall, which was a luxury they could not afford. The increased expenditures were not followed by an increase in revenue, and the company discovered that its newly acquired capital reserve was not a bottomless pit. Stock initially selling at $4 per unit of two shares and a warrant, fell with the company's fortunes and hit a low of $1.50 per unit.

In November of the same year, Steve Prato received a call from Doug, Gardner-Smith, and Ekberg. The company was about out of money and there was rioting between the management and Doug Wilson. "Steve, can you help us?" said Gardner-Smith, who was preparing to leave on a cruise. "You can have my car and my house in Coronado, just come out here and straighten things out." Prato was faced with a tough decision; he knew how to run an investment business, but not a fashion design company. Here was a client who represented his first underwriting, on which he put his company's name and reputation on the prospectus. Here, also, was a client in whom he invested hundreds of thousands of dollars of his investors money on the faith that Doug Wilson Studios, Inc. was a good deal.

Prato had no choice—he had to try to save the company. Wilson and Prato met the next day. Wilson explained how he lost faith in his management and that he feared that now he would never get those sportswear designs off the sketchbooks and into the department stores. Prato did some digging into the financial statements and found that liabilities actually exceeded assets and that cash was very low. Prato and Wilson agreed; it was time to sharpen the axe and let it fall. In the next three months, heads rolled out alongside excess overhead. Prato eliminated the entire management group and reduced the staff by over 60 percent. Wilson's time was now free from internal struggles and endless meetings and he was now able to focus on what he knew best: creating and designing. All efforts were focused on eliminating overhead and increasing sales. What little cash that could be mustered was provided to support the sales offices in New York and Los Angeles that were generating all the revenue.

In a recent fashion show for the Denver investment community, where Doug unveiled his much-awaited new line of sportswear, Wilson presented a brief series of slides before the show to explain how the company was able to recover from its misfortune: "Here is a picture of our management staff," said Wilson, pointing to a slide of gorillas in the San Diego Zoo, "which Steve Prato fired when he came to La Jolla." "Here is a picture of our lovely corporate office, which

Steve Prato closed when he came to La Jolla," he continued. "Here is a picture of our retail store in downtown La Jolla, which Steve closed. Here is a picture of our retail store in the University Towne Shopping Center, which Steve also closed. And finally, here are our smaller offices and our reduced, but happy and ambitious staff, who are hard at work selling my new creations, which you are about to see."

Wilson presented his main sleepwear line, which for the past two years have been the main source of sales for the company. Wilson's line of nightshirts for young women and teens resemble oversized football jerseys. They are emblazoned with cute serigraphs of teddy bears, ducks, and penguins and some carry phrases, such as, "Studying, Do Not Disturb—except in case of emergency or party," "Make Me Late for Breakfast," and, "I was a Good Girl—but I've reformed." These shirts were a big hit for many department stores across the country. Doug Wilson then presented his new line of nightshirts with a series of pictures of bears on the front with lettering stating, "Beary Tired."

With overhead cut by more than 60 percent and sales growth up by over 100 percent to the $5 million annual level, the company was able to obtain enough cash through internal operations to finance Wilson's exciting new lines of sportswear. Doug Wilson refers to his line of sportswear as "Cartoon Clothes." Wilson says that his clothes try to provide the freedom, color, and excitement that young women enjoy with Esprit with the addition of Wilson's fun and savoir-faire design style. Wilson's new sportwear line includes brightly colored "cafe shirts" reminiscent of the 1950s diner look, but with added flair and color. There's a complete line of tops, shorts, slacks, skirts, and jumpsuits for women featuring a cast of duck characters, including a movie star, producer, and director.

Wilson's up, campy new look has caught on. Bloomingdale's and Macy's immediately signed on to carry the line, and C. Itoh and Company, a major Japanese trading company, will be distributing the Doug Wilson line in Japan. Says Wilson:

"The creativity was always there but management wasn't. A lot of people thought we were history when we had our problems. It was so bad that the management fired agreed to give back their stock in exchange for severance pay, thinking that the stock would be valueless." But Wilson never gave up, and as a result, his designer sportswear collection is now a reality. Says Prato, "Crisis situations also provide the best opportunity; the people who believed in us, who kept buying the stock as it fell, will now make nice profits on their investment. As for the company, it is a lot stronger now than ever before because the crises forced us to clean up our act—we are running very lean and mean now."

After a string of losing quarters, the company is now reporting profits. Sales, which have increased from $2.5 million to $5 million in one year, are expected to go beyond $10 million in 1987. "We expect sales to go a lot further than our 1987 projection," says Wilson, "but because we are a public company, we have to be conservative on our projections."

Whether Wilson will become the next Ralph Lauren or Liz Claiborne is an issue that only time will tell, but what is sure is that he is an exciting idea man and designer who has proven he is here to stay. His story represents a number of valuable lessons that hopefully will prevent other budding young entrepreneurs from repeating similar mistakes. Experience sometimes requires that we make our own mistakes, but wisdom is our ability to learn from the mistakes of others.

JOSHUA BEREN

JOSHUA BEREN OF CCT, INC.

"We are known as the company that can take an AT&T computer and make it do anything you want it to do."

Joshua (Josh) Beren, 24, has lived through more entrepreneurial endeavors and pitfalls than most men twice his age. Since the age of 17 he has established a number of high-tech, service-related businesses to pay his way through college, built a company that went from $100,000 to $18 million within three years, survived a bitter partnership breakup, and founded a new company that is currently running at a $22 million annualized sales rate. Oh, and I should add that somewhere along the way he also has found the time to become an ordained rabbi, a private pilot, an accomplished weightlifter, a first-aid-squad captain, and the father of three children (a fourth is on the way). A close-cropped, full-face beard makes him appear older than his 24 years. But it is his youth that serves to underscore the fact the he is a chronic overachiever. Indeed, there's more to Beren and his company, Concepts in Computer Technology (CCT), than that which meets the eye.

CCT opened its doors in October of 1985 after Beren and a former partner parted company, both figuratively and literally. Starting a new company was to Josh, in many ways, just another milestone in a life that is filled with them. Prior to founding CCT, Josh had started and successfully run several service-oriented businesses, making his debut into the business world at the ripe old age of 17 to pay his way through college. An easy-going disposition, bright smile, and quick wit belie Beren's shrewd business sense while making him immediately likeable to both vendors and customers alike.

His Lakewood, New Jersey-based company is one of the country's most dynamic value-added-resellers (VARs) of AT&T computer systems, in addition to being a full-service system integrator and configurator. Beren has aggressive short- and long-term plans for CCT's continued growth and expansion, but to fully appreciate his ambitious forecasts we would do well to look at his past track record.

Josh was born of Orthodox Jewish parents in Brooklyn, New York, lived a few years of his early childhood in Denver, Colorado, and moved back to Brooklyn at age 10. He attended high school in Philadelphia and enrolled in rabbinical college in Lakewood, New Jersey, with the distinction of being the youngest member of the Yeshiva—he was then 17 years old.

His entrepreneurial spirit had its beginnings and was nurtured during his childhood by watching and, subsequently, learning from his father's example. The senior Beren was the founder of Beren Energy Corporation of Denver, a highly successful oil "wildcatting" and development company.

Throughout the primary and secondary grades, Josh proved to be an excellent student with a natural aptitude for learning and scholarly self-discipline. He also displayed a marked penchant for electronics and an insatiable curiosity about how things worked, even from early childhood.

Beren is, and always has been, a highly self-motivated person who believes strongly in making it on his own, as evidenced by the fact that he worked his way through college, although he didn't have to. He quickly realized that he could capitalize on his electronics knowledge and prowess. With innate marketing savvy, he converted his hobby interests into tuition and living money by doing home and car alarm and stereo installations throughout Lakewood and surrounding areas. This first venture was highly successful for the young rabbinical student.

Early to identify and define potential profit centers, Beren cofounded a company that sold and installed automatic telephone dialing systems; he was 18 when he launched this venture. Reflecting back on that era, Josh recalled their seat-of-the-pants production methods with a smile, saying, "We bought parts and put together the systems." The business got off to a brisk start and grew rapidly, but he withdrew from the partnership a year later to marry and start a family while completing his education. He retained the Digitel Systems company name to cover his computer consulting ventures.

Josh's former partner continued on with the business trading under the name Digitel Telecom Systems, and remains a close friend to this day. The company has prospered into a 75-employee organization with service representatives in 45 major U.S. cities and has garnered national contracts for the installation and service of long distance calling systems.

Josh graduated with a rabbinical degree, and as his family continued to grow, so did his social consciousness and community involvement. The young rabbi organized a first-aid squad for Lakewood's Jewish community, naming it *Hatzolah*, which means "rescue" in Hebrew. He designed the radio-dispatching system for *Hatzolah* and this same system was later used for other first-aid squads in the New York area as well. Beren is as active as ever, keeping a hand-held two-way radio constantly within hearing range throughout the business day (three of his employees are also members of the first-aid squad, and they all respond to calls when needed). As the squad's founder, chairman, and captain, Josh is justifiably proud of *Hatzolah*'s fast response time of two to four minutes.

He was also an influential force who contributed technical input toward the organization of "ITT," the Institute of Torah and Technology, on whose board of directors he serves as vice president. ITT was modeled after Boys' Town, a school in Jerusalem, which teaches young people ancient Jewish law along with modern computer technology.

He continued going to school at night after receiving his rabbinical degree, and started consulting on computer programming problems for local businessmen. He established his pattern of long work hours back in those days, confiding, "I would work from nine in the morning until about four-thirty in the afternoon. Then I would attend yeshiva from four-thirty until nine in the evening. Occasionally, when things got hectic, I'd go back to the office until the early hours of the morning."

Recalling how he managed to turn another hobby into a profitable full-time venture, he says, "My computer business actually started on an all-volunteer basis—until I decided I might as well make money from it."

Digitel Systems limped along for the first year and a half, providing computer consulting services and designing programs for local businesses. Josh became intrigued with AT&T's then-new UNIX multiuser operating system and studied it intently. Always the perpetually curious tinkerer, he soon started playing "mix and match" and software and hardware components, linking AT&T items with those of other manufacturers in an effort to establish compatability. As usual, he was highly successful and later designed entire systems selecting componentry that would produce the most efficient combinations, regardless of manufacturer. He developed a real flair for integration and interfacing, as well as an intimate knowledge of UNIX and its nuances.

Digitel wasn't prospering at the rate that Beren felt it had the potential for, so he took a serious look at what the company needed in order to grow at the pace he projected. Josh decided to handle the technical side of the company himself and find someone to handle sales. In February 1984, he took on a partner and formed a new company. This decision was to have a profound effect on the shape of things to come.

Beren and his new partner attended the 1984 COMDEX (Computer Dealer Exposition) computer trade show and slipped past a guard one night after regular show hours to talk to the AT&T exhibitors who were closing down their booth. Josh recalls, "We started talking about UNIX. I knew things about UNIX that most people didn't know, and that impressed them enough to invite us to a private AT&T party later that night." They met more AT&T executives at the party and put the wheels in motion to secure official status as a Value Added Reseller (VAR) of AT&T's UNIX computer systems and equipment by the end of the evening.

Beren and company, with the blessings of AT&T, immediately embarked on a campaign to "bundle" AT&T equipment with products of their own design as well as those of other manufacturers, reselling complete systems with software specifically conceived and written for the clients' needs.

The new company did very well, building up to annual sales of over $18 million, but disagreements between the two partners ensued regarding making contractual commitments that Beren believed could not realistically be met. Josh recounted an incident involving a large contract with a major financial brokerage firm to develop a UNIX-based computer system for their offices in which his partner committed to delivering in three months a system that Josh thought would have taken three years to develop. A subtle flush of controlled emotion was evident as Josh spoke of the situation, which worsened steadily between himself and his former partner. The two men could not reconcile their differences and decided to go their separate ways. Josh turned over his interest in the company for under $250,000 in cash and equipment, feeling relieved to be disassociated from it. "I would have left for nothing," he states candidly. "I didn't want my name associated with his anymore. Besides, the real value was not the company—it was the people and the technology."

Beren had both, and they came with him as he struck out on his own. On October 15, 1985, Concepts in Computer Technology, was founded. The same day he sold his interest in the former venture. "When I left that day, all the employees quit and joined me, with the exception of my partner's brother and the receptionist."

Josh immediately rallied his forces, put together a plan of action and embarked on it. The first order of business was reestablishing his business relationships and obtaining a $1 million line of credit so he could purchase equipment and components in volume; Beren had established a good rapport with several banks, and he obtained the necessary letters of credit based on their faith in him. Like his employees and banks, Josh's vendors also exhibited their confidence in his direction and extended him 30-day credit lines based entirely on handshakes and good faith.

Everyone's faith has been rewarded—the company did over $1.7 million by its third month in business and established an escalating sales pattern that has shown no signs of letting up.

Beren is quick to attribute a large portion of the company's success to his staff. "We have super-dedicated employees; you'll see lots of people working here past ten or eleven at night besides myself." His people certainly appear to be highly motivated and quite content, holding their chief in high esteem. Anyone visiting CCT immediately gets the impression that the people working there *like* what they're doing; their enthusiasm is evident.

Beren's staff is up to 16 employees (as of this writing), and Josh is currently on the look-out for some more good people. In addition to the 3,500 square feet of office space the company occupies, CCT has also leased a 5,000-square-foot warehouse at a separate location in Lakewood. The current space arrangement is only a stop-gap measure, according to Josh, until a suitable site providing more square footage can be found and leased or, preferably, purchased by the company.

CCT has expanded and branched the scope of its operations to include the development and packaging of several "personalized" UNIX-based systems in addition to developing, manufacturing, and marketing its own products. A particularly viable product area for CCT has been manufacturing its own line of mass storage devices and hard-disk subsystems, selling them to system assemblers and manufacturers on a private-label basis. CCT also expects to be marketing its own hard-disk-on-a-card for personal computers by the time this is in print.

Beren's strategy for the company's growth can be generally outlined in two key areas:

1. *Offer the best value.* That means using premium elements at minimal markup to produce and deliver the completed

system. Though this practice results in a smaller profit margin, it develops business while providing cash flow and higher overall sales volume, both essential to long-term growth. An added advantage of delivering superior value is that it provides a solid means of getting the corporate foot in the door with new account leads.

2. *Purchase in volume whenever possible.* This results in increased volume and lower per-unit cost, which permits the company to offer more competitive pricing for its own systems.

This strategy has put CCT in the forefront among system integrators, and Beren is considering expanding his market share by opening offices in Atlanta, Los Angeles, Dallas, Chicago, and other major cities. The company is also vigorously engaged in a marketing campaign that contacts *Fortune 500* companies directly regarding the design, configuration, and installation of UNIX-based systems to fit their specific needs. CCT has done exceedingly well in providing complete turn-key systems to numerous firms in the New York–New Jersey–Pennsylvania metropolitan areas.

Josh's extended long-range plans include establishing a separate subsidiary to provide technical and repair service for computer equipment on a nationwide basis. He also eyes the prospects of going public with CCT furtively, saying, "The public trading of our stock will be a big incentive for our staff."

As Beren goes on to explain the reasons for going public, the phone suddenly rings. "What?" exclaims Beren. "Don't worry, I'll work on the conversion. I told you, I'll handle the conversion." He sits and listens for a while and then smiles. "Don't worry, I'll handle your wife, too. I'm good at talking to wives."

I looked at my watch and said, "Josh, it's eight-thirty at night. Are you now going to play rabbi and convert someone?"

"No, not at all," said Beren. "I was just talking to one of my employees who was staying late to write up a proposal.

He wants to make sure I can convert Lotus 1-2-3 for a personal computer so it can access the 20-20 files for an AT&T 3BS computer. I told him I could, and then his next problem was his fear of coming home late and having his wife kill him for being late again. I told him, I'll handle that too." Beren then smiles and looks toward the heavens and says, "Believe me when I say I am good at talking to wives. I have had a lot of practice explaining why I have to come home late to my own."

TED LEONSIS

TED LEONSIS
OF REDGATE
COMMUNICATIONS
CORPORATION

You would think that selling your company for millions of dollars before reaching the age of 30 would be the highlight of your career, but for Leonsis it soon turned out to be quite the opposite.

"**M**y first experience as an entrepreneur was a failure. I started my first business while attending college at Georgetown during the bicentennial. I sold red, white, and blue snowcones. My two partners were rich and unmotivated; I was hungry but inexperienced—it was a miserable failure." Ted Leonsis is able to reflect on his past with a smile because he realized the value of "getting scarred" in a small way early in his career. "The few thousand dollars I lost on my first experience," says Leonsis, "saved me tens of thousands in mistakes I didn't repeat later on." Leonsis evidently learned well, because he later recovered from his setback to build one of the fastest growing marketing communications companies in the country. His success has won such accolades from his industry as: "One of the few idea men in the industry," *INFO WORLD*. "One of the industry's few true 'movers and shakers,' " *Publisher's Weekly*.

Leonsis graduated first in his class from Georgetown at age 20 and started work with Wang as a copy editor. In two years he became advertising manager for the company's computer and word processing departments, and later started the company's public relations department. Leonsis left Wang at 25 and moved to Florida to join Harris Corporation as a director of marketing communications.

But it wasn't long before the entrepreneurial bug bit Leonsis again. After 18 months with Harris, Leonsis got an idea for a new company. "When IBM produced the PC I smelled opportunity. I went down to Boca Raton, and after seeing the potential I decided to start a software directory for the PC industry." So at 26, Leonsis founded Redgate Publishing, which published *LIST*, a personal computer software magazine/ catalog in January of 1982, with $1 million in venture capital provided by E.F. Hutton.

E.F. Hutton was impressed by Leonsis's business plan and agreed to pay the $1 million for 40 percent of the company. "At the time there was a frenzy in the market and magazines were selling at 20 to 30 times earnings" said Leonsis. Leonsis also learned from his past mistakes and teamed up with an experienced, hard-working industry veteran, Joe Weibel, who joined him as an equal partner. "Joe was 48; I needed Joe for credibility with customers, bankers, and investors. One good bit of advice is team up early with experienced people who are older and wiser than yourself." Leonsis positioned Redgate publishing to be the entrepreneurial leader in the computer software magazine field. In addition to publishing *LIST*, Redgate developed a newsletter and a series of computer software book contracts with Warner Books.

In August of 1983, Redgate Publishing sold to International Thomson Business Press for $15 million. E.F. Hutton cashed out for $4 million on their $1 million investment. Leonsis and his partner split $6 million equally. The remainder of the deal was made in a series of installment payments over a period of five years.

You would think that selling your company for millions of dollars before reaching the age of 30 would be the highlight of your career, but for Leonsis it soon turned out to be quite the opposite. "Thomson told us that they could do things better and make us more publishing oriented. I wanted to make more money by presenting more information to the computer industry; they believed they could simply make more money by increasing our overhead and volume. Thomson reasoned that if we could make $400,000 profit with two issues of *LIST* a year, we could make $2.4 million in profit with a monthly issue of *LIST*." The difference was that a monthly magazine needs more subscribers and editorial people. It also generated a lot more expenses and overhead. Leonsis saw a terrible difference in philosophy between his company and the new owners. Redgates' employees saw themselves transformed in the public's eye from a "loose bunch of successful guys to a bunch of corporate failures."

Redgate went from a profit to a loss in the first year after its acquisition. In the second year, in the midst of the computer slump, it broke even. In the third year Thomson had a management change, and in October of 1985 Leonsis decided to take action. "I got mad and bought the company back from them."

If lesson number one for Leonsis was "hire experienced people," then lesson number two was clearly "buy low, sell high, and buy back even cheaper." Leonsis sold his company at 15 times earnings and repurchased the company for five times earnings, which was considerably less than the earnings in its prior profitable years. Leonsis now owns 65 percent of Redgate Publishing, which he has renamed Redgate Communications Corporation. The remaining stock is shared with his two other partners, Alfred Mandel, who runs the West Coast office, and Jeff Parson, his chief financial officer. Within one year Leonsis and his partners took their staff of 20, which was producing $3 million in revenue, to one of 40, producing over $8 million in revenues with an estimated 12 percent pretax profit. Leonsis is shooting for $12 million in revenues for 1987.

Leonsis changed Redgate's name to reflect the full range of services they planned to offer to their clients and to the marketplace. Redgate Communications Corporation is a full-service marketing communications company offering advertising, public relations, and a publications agency all rolled into one. Redgate has established the company by focusing on the market niche. They are one of the only full-service communication and publishing agencies in the high tech field. Their clients benefit by not having to endure the costs of establishing three or four separate budgets for their marketing, publishing, and advertising requirements and by saving a great deal of time by dealing with one vendor for all their communications needs. Redgate's clients include Apple,

Commodore, Compaq, CCI, Coyne Kalojian, Kodak, Harris, Hewlett-Packard, Motorola, Texas Instruments, Wang, Warner Communications, Private Satellite Networks, Contel, Concurrent Computer Corp., Lotus Development Corp., and Xerox Information Systems.

Redgate still works on its original base business, which was and still is publishing. It continues to publish magazines for the computer field: *The MacIntosh Buyer's Guide*, *The Apple II Review*, *The Amiga Buyers Guide* and *COMPAQ* magazine. Redgate is currently working on producing a special section on America's space effort for *Forbes* magazine and plans to add aerospace technology as a field of expertise. Redgate will market and sell it through seminars, videos, conferences, publications, and consulting. (Leonsis has also written and published several books for Warner Communications and is working on a new book concerning the people behind the IBM PC.) The advertising and marketing expertise that Redgate developed to produce its own magazines has enabled it not only to contract to produce magazines for outside clients but also to market its services as a public relations and advertising agency. According to Leonsis, the new Redgate Communications will continue to capitalize on its own internal expertise and resources by moving into other areas of technology outside of the computer industry.

Even with all his success, Leonsis has still managed to keep his sense of humor as well as his humility. In addition to starting a venture capital fund for collegiate entrepreneurs, Leonsis founded a new company, *Three Ethnics and a Wasp*, to produce a board game called *"Only In New York."* Recently Leonsis spoke at an entrepreneurship conference at his alma mater, Georgetown University, and told the audience that "although today people try to make entrepreneurs into rock stars, really a lot of us are just plain assholes." Leonsis also mused that he was surprised that people teach entrepreneurship.

Now 30, Leonsis may find that his third great lesson will be to "buy low, sell high, buy back even cheaper, and sell

even higher." His profitable company is positioning itself for
either a public offering or possibly a merger or acquisition.
"We want to be a $50 million business," says Leonsis. Leonsis
has trained himself to think big. "In marketing, the cost of
comfort is impact. Whenever we have done marketing for a
client we go for the great idea, not the comfortable idea. We
do this for ourselves as well. We spent more than half of our
$1 million of funding from Hutton on advertising. We ran
ads in the *Wall Street Journal* and *Inc*. We were perceived as
a big company. Thomson saw these ads and decided to buy
us rather than compete with us." Leonsis is a firm believer
in "acting big," because if you market yourself as big and
are perceived by your clients that way it soon becomes a self-
fulfilling prophecy.

The following are other key lessons that Leonsis has learned.

1. If you are motivated only by money, you will be unhappy
   and you will fail in the long term.
2. Do not think that "the experts" are always smarter than
   you. Entrepreneurs succeed by creating the innovations
   that the experts do not believe are possible.
3. Get a real strong person in the CFO position and give
   him stock incentive so he is motivated and don't mess
   around in his area. Entrepreneurs tend to be very weak
   and disorganized with numbers, and they need a strong
   hands-on financial manager to keep them out of trouble.
4. Delegate authority and hire people smarter than yourself.
   You will want to be able to take vacations.
5. Have a clear picture of what you are doing. Ask yourself
   what business are you in and make sure you are in it.
6. Do not get married to your idea. "*LIST*, being the *TV
   Guide* for software, was a great idea in 1982 but a terrible
   idea for 1986. If I was married to the idea, I would be
   out of business right now rather than being in a successful
   diversified company." Be flexible.

7. Don't take yourself too seriously. "I have watched myself
   go from a genius to an asshole to a genius too quickly
   in the press." You have to believe in yourself and don't
   get a false sense of self-worth.

Perhaps the last point sums up the basis for Leonsis's
business philosophy. By being open and honest with yourself,
you will continue to grow and be creative, and a belief in
your own success is a self-fulfilling prophecy. Leonsis is one
who truly believes.

LESSONS LEARNED FROM THE DYNAMOS

The two greatest lessons that I have learned in business were taught to me by the same person. They were learned the hard way, from the man who delivered my first major defeat. He was a wise, old Wall Street tycoon who abruptly woke me up to the real world.

I was a cocky young entrepreneur who had had the good fortune of experiencing success at an early age. After succeeding in my previous ventures, I became involved as an investor in another company in the Silicon Valley. I was 22 years old when I worked with the company to help them go public on Wall Street.

I thought I had the Midas touch. I was soon to be blessed with my first failure, at an early age. After filing three new prospectuses during a period of over seven months and spending over $100,000 in underwriting related fees, my Wall Street friend decided to back away from the deal. We thought we had a firm commitment for the underwriting; we learned later that the commitment was secondary to what the underwriter thought the stock would do in the marketplace at that given time. Wall Street plays by its own rules and often these rules are very unforgiving.

We were devastated by the losses, because we had believed the earlier assurances that the deal would go through and had taken no action to prepare ourselves for the consequences of its not doing so.

Faced with mounting losses, I had to immediately look toward obtaining private financing for the fledgling enterprise. After months of hard work, not to mention precarious negotiations with both investors and the banks, we obtained the financing and eventually the company prospered. The experience opened my eyes to the realistic necessity of anticipating failure, particularly my own, and learning how to correctly plan for it and manage my risks. Jay Jordan said it: "The best thing that can happen to an entrepreneur is to have a failure of magnitude early in life." Dynamo Ted Leonsis echoed it: "Get scarred early." Failure is as much a part of life as success. See to it that you are able to learn from both experiences.

Although I suffered great hardship because of the first lesson this Wall Street tycoon taught me, I can't help but admire him for the way he taught me my second and most important lesson. Like a father talking to his son, he would often say to me, "Success is a self-fulfilling prophecy." Deals get sold because they're "hot," hot deals are created by deal makers convincing the buyers that the stocks are in demand. You don't sit back and hope for your success. You, and only you, have to make it happen.

No one wants to buy a stock if he feels it is too easy to obtain, because that means the price won't be bid up by an oversubscription of demand. Obviously, when you first start to market your product or your stock it couldn't possibly be in hot demand; you have to create the sense of urgency by telling them that the deal is hot. As you persist in doing this, the deal eventually becomes hot. Hence, your prophesy is fulfilled.

Imparting a sense of urgency about your success to everything you do is something the dynamos talk about frequently. One of the problems I have always found in myself, as well as in many other entrepreneurs, is our well-developed propensity to exaggerate. I guess we would like to think our exaggerations are a function of our ability to see our future clearly. We often really believe we are "working toward $3 million in sales" after we have just succeeded in chalking up our first. Often our bold and brash statements force us to commit ourselves to achieving those stated goals. We have to fulfill our prophecy or worry about encountering criticism or being proven wrong. Although a hard cold sense of reality is very important in business, what makes entrepreneurs special is that they have the self-confidence to openly admit their bold dreams and, hence work toward them. Says Leonsis, "Unspectacular achievements are not worth achieving."

If both experiencing failure and overcoming your fear of it is important, and commiting yourself to fulfill your personal prophecy of success is another major tenet, what are the other key lessons we can learn from the dynamos—lessons that will benefit us in our own lives, both in our business and professional careers?

Of course, there are many more lessons to be learned. It probably would be impossible for us to cover each and every one of them in detail without selling you an encyclopedia instead of a one-volume book. There are, however, seven areas of general advice that recur throughout the book:

1. *Choose a field or industry and position yourself for success.* Success will not just sneak up on you one day, bite you on the ass, and announce that it has arrived. You have to *position* yourself for success. "Positioning" is the process by which we place ourself in a situation where we are aware of opportunities and can participate in them. An opportunity will not find you when you are locked in a closet. Nor will it come rapping on the

door behind which you are chained to a desk in a job where you don't have the freedom or time to circulate with people in your industry.

If you are committed to starting your own business, the best way to position yourself for opportunities is simply to do it! Start your company, put your shingle outside your door, let people know you're in business, and make sure you let the big people in the industry know who you are and what you do. The best way to choose a field or industry for yourself, according to real estate dynamo David Solomon, is "stick to what you know and focus your energies on succeeding in one thing." It is hard to be positioned to succeed in any given field or industry if you spread yourself too thin, because when the time comes to move on a hot opportunity, you most likely will not have the resources, the time, or the liquidity to follow through on it.

2. *Market and leverage your time, money, and ability.* If there are any true secrets to success, they may be those that evolve from an ability to "work smart," rather than simply working hard. Hard work is necessary, but if hard work alone were the only factor required for success, manual laborers would all be millionaires!

The secret of working smart are in this book. If you missed them, reread it. Pay particular attention to the unit on leverage. Leverage your resources so you can get the most from your time, money, and ability.

Working smart also requires that you limit your risks. Never bet everything on one throw of the dice. Learn how to motivate and hire good people, and you will surely grow beyond your individual abilities. Build an organization that is committed to making great achievements and take on partners, financiers, or advisors when necessary so you can learn painlessly to grow to the next level of your success.

3. *Be persistent—never take "no" for an answer.* Persistence separates the winners from the losers. Losers give up;

winners continue to persist toward a successful conclusion. However, there is a difference between persistence and blind stubbornness. Stubborn people are persistent in a negative way. They are not open-minded and thus don't view reality clearly.

One of the worst things a stubborn entrepreneur can do is persist in sinking with a ship that was never meant to sail. Even after making your initial investment, if you find your business idea is not valid, by all means, when the ship starts to sink, don't cling, jump! Learn to accept small losses cheerfully as a fact of life. Don't throw good money after bad or you will surely go down.

Most entrepreneurs fail a few times before experiencing their ultimate success. The positive side of their persistence allows them to keep trying until they finally succeed. They don't allow stubbornness to chain them to one failure.

Expect to experience several setbacks and even a few failures while traveling toward success. Positive persistence in working toward success in every way you can will never leave you with the sad feeling in the pit of your stomach that tells you it's too late, that you didn't try hard enough.

4. *Patience.* In the end it's not who ran the fastest at the starting gate that counts, it's who crosses the finish line first. Don't ever count your chips, or your peers or competitors, while they're on the table. Real success shows in the person who can hold onto the money after the game is over.

Many times both entrepreneurs and deal makers will use the phrase "you've got to stay at the table." The table is really your business, or remaining independent, both financially and otherwise as a deal maker so you can continue to put together deals for your own account rather than for others. Clearly, if you go out of business or cannot survive without a salary by waiting for your deals to close, you have "left the table" and cannot continue to "play the game." Maintaining your position at the table is therefore as important as placing yourself there initially. I have found, particularly in the investment banking and deal-making business, that during slow periods in the market, when many firms and deal makers went out of business because they could not support their overhead, the few firms and individuals that remained and simply survived through the bad times were the ones who were best positioned to get a jump on the market the minute things turned around. Patience, persistence, and perseverance will alert you to the next opportunity—which may be just around the corner. Even if some deals initially seem to pass you by, my experience has been that if you just stay at the table they often eventually come back to you.

5. *Self-confidence and a strong ego* are healthy in business as long as you can control your ego rather than letting it control you. Your ego should be a motivator, not a troublemaker. Having confidence in yourself is important to success, says Solomon. "Self-confidence helps you endure hardship. . . . I never would have made it in this business if I didn't have a big ego." Optimism means expecting the best, but confidence means knowing how you will handle the worst.

6. *Always be creative and never stop dreaming.* Brett Davis said, "It is an entrepreneur's divine right to dream." He could not have been more correct. Dreams are just the beginnings of enterprises to come. They are also the source of many of our new ideas to improve our present business operations. Remember that the creative process should not end after you have opened your doors for business. Creativity is as important in keeping the business maintained and growing as it is to establish it initially.

7. *Enjoy your success.* There are a few entrepreneurs, including some whom I interviewed, who try to find their

happiness in money. Up to a certain point, money is very much a necessity of life. But after you achieve a certain level of success it should be more of a means to keep score in a game you continue to enjoy playing. Business should be looked upon as a game you enjoy. A healthy attitude is never take yourself too seriously. No matter how rich you get, your stomach won't be able to digest more steaks than you can eat, and you won't be able to drive more than one car at the same time, regardless of how many you own. You have to be happy with who you are and what you are doing, now and in the future. Simply stated, money will not provide happiness. Money will provide comfort, freedom from many common daily worries, and perhaps even a very luxurious lifestyle, but not happiness.

Don't get me wrong. Money doesn't necessarily buy misery, either. Contrary to some stereotypes, there are some very happy and well-adjusted millionaires. You've just read about a number of them. Their happiness is clearly more a function of their personal philosophy of life and their willingness to keep life in perspective than of their net worth. They work hard because they enjoy challenge and excitement. Money itself is not the end. Yes, it's a nice prize to reward success; however, the main motivator of the dynamos is their enjoyment of the independence, freedom, creativity, and opportunity that makes their lives as entrepreneurs both interesting and rewarding.

People who worship money are not happy. I should know; as an author I have interviewed a few of them and as an investment banker I have worked with more than a few as well. I was astonished by the statements of one dynamo (whose story was later deleted from the book at her request) who questioned why I chose to make donations to charity instead of buying a new car or acquiring a summer house.

I would even go so far as to say that I don't completely trust people who only worship money, because they

have no other laws that guide them either in business
or in life. It's important for people to believe in something,
in themselves as well as in a system of values that make
us what we are. It's important to all our futures that
money is not always used as our ultimate goal. When
faced with a choice, it will always be better to make a
few dollars less in order to maintain our ability to drink
clean water and breathe clean air. People who only worship money would not make this choice and will soon
harm others as well as themselves.

Keep things in perspective and enjoy your success.
Sometimes it is better to make a few dollars less and
leave the table with a smile on your face, knowing that
although you have succeeded you have still left some
money on the table to share your wealth and profits
with others. In the long run you will come out ahead
because people will want to continue to do business
with others who share. You will then go through life
not only making more successful deals, but more true
friends as well. Enjoy your success!

THE ACE 100—
The Top 100
Entrepreneurs
in the United States
Under 30

The following list ranks the top 100 entrepreneurs under 30 according to their estimated gross sales over the past 12 months. This list was initially prepared by the Association of College Entrepreneurs. During my research for the *Dynamos* I discovered numerous new additions to the list, which I have included. Whereas the previous ACE 100 list had a cutoff point of $250,000 in gross sales, our updated version has a cutoff point at $485,000. The reader should note that the information was obtained in 1986 prior to publication, so we can expect gross sales, number of employees, and other factors including age to change over time. Obviously, both age and gross sales will affect the present ACE 100's future positioning on the list. For ease of usage, I have listed the information in the following order: Name, Affiliation, Industry, Present Age, Startup Date, Startup Age, Education, Gross Sales, and Number of Employees.

To those planning to participate in an entrepreneurial endeavor, I wish you luck in joining the next update of the ACE 100.

1. Steven Jobs
   Apple Computer
   Personal Computer
   Cupertino, CA
   30
   January 1977
   22
   One Semester at Reed College
   $1,900,000,000
   5200

2. Brett Davis
   Stockton Savings Assoc./ Troy Nichols
   Mortgage Bank
   Banking/Financial Services
   Dallas, TX, Monroe, LA
   27
   February 1984 (Acquired)
   25
   High School equivalency
   $845,000,000
   700

3. Mark Hughes
   Herbal Life
   Direct Sales
   Inglenook, CA
   30
   February 1980
   23
   High school graduate
   $512,000,000
   700,000

4. William H. Gates III
   Microsoft Corp.

Computer Software
Bellview, WA
30
January 1975
20
Harvard University
$140,000,000
900+

5. Debrah L. Charatan
   Bach Realty Inc.
   Real Estate Brokerage
   New York, NY
   28
   May 1980
   BA Baruch College
   $100,000,000
   35

6. Michael Dell
   PC's Limited
   Personal Computer
   Austin, TX
   20
   May 1984
   18
   University of Texas (4 Semesters)
   $80,000,000
   138

7. Debbi Fields
   Mrs. Fields Cookies
   Food
   Park City, UT
   29
   1977
   20

Foothills College
$80,000,000
1,500

8. Xavier Roberts
Original Appalachian Art-
works, Inc.
Toy/Dolls
Cleveland, CA
30
August 1978
24
Truett McConnell College
(1½ years, no degree)
$40,000,000
300

9. Barron Thomas
Barron Thomas Aviation
Aircraft
Dallas, TX
29
1978
20
So. Methodist University,
no degree
$40,000,000
1

10. Mr. Robert Thomson
Red Shaw, Inc.
Insurance
Pittsburgh, PA
29
1978
20
BS, Nuclear Physics,
Carnegie-Mellon Univer-

sity, CPCU
$40,000,000
300

11. David Fishof
David Fishof Productions,
Inc.
Film Productions
New York, NY
30
June 1976
20
Bernard Baruch, BA Sci-
ence
$25,000,000–$30,000,000
8

12. Joshua Beren
CCT
Computer Systems Dis-
tributing
Lakewood, NJ
24
October 15, 1985
23
Graduate Rabbinical Col-
lege, Lakewood, NJ
$22,000,000
16

13. Jay Adoni
Admos Shoe Corporation
Shoe Manufacturing
Brooklyn, NY
27
May 1978
19
3 years of high school,

no diploma

-$20,000,000

250

14. Sophia Collier
American Natural Beverage Corp.
Soft Drink
New York, NY
30
1977
22
Verde Valley High School
$20,000,000
50

15. Silvano DiGenova
Tangible Investments of America, Inc.
Investment Company
Philadelphia, PA
24
1983
21
Three years at Wharton School of Business
$20,000,000
10

16. Steve Schussler
Juke Box Saturday Night
Music/Entertainment
Chicago, IL
30
September 1980
25
2 years of college
$18,000,000
350

17. Kevin Curran
Doug Macrae
General Computer
Computer Hard Disk Manufacturers
Cambridge, MA
27/27
1981
22/22
Massachusetts Institute of Technology, completing education
$18,000,000
1030

18. Richard Berman
Steve Berman
Motormite Mfg., Inc.
Auto Parts
Huntington Valley, PA
29/36
November 1978
23/20
Graduate of University of Pennsylvania/2 years at Temple University
$17,240,000
200

19. Jimmy C. Calano
Careertrack Inc.
Education
Boulder, CO
28
1982
24
University of Colorado, 1979 Graduate

$15,000,000
100

20. Ginnie J. Johansen
Ginnie Johansen, Inc.
Fashion
Dallas, TX
25
January 1978
18
Sophie Newcomp 2 years/
Southern Methodist Uni-
versity, 2 ½ years part
time, degree uncom-
pleted
$11,000,000
115

21. William M. Haney III
Fuel Tech Inc.
Energy
Stamford, CT
23
June 1981
18
Portsmouth Abby/Har-
vard College
$11,000,000
140

22. Steven Kirsch
Mouse Systems Corp.
Computer
Santa Clara, CA
29
July 1982
27
Massachusetts Institute of
Technology, MD Electri-

cal Engineering/Massa-
cusetts Institute of Technology, BD Electrical
Engineering
$10,500,000
78

23. David Schlessinger
Encore Books
Book sales
Philadelphia, PA
30
1974
18
University of Pennsylva-
nia, degree uncompleted
$10,000,000
150–200

24. Brandt Hibbs
Hibbs International Busi-
ness Brokerage Services,
Inc.
Financial Service
Fairfax, VA
19
1983
16
High school graduate
$10,000,000
11

25. Sharon Corr
R. J. Corr Naturals
Soft Drink
Chicago, IL
29
1978
20

BS Radiology, General
Science: Duke University
$10,000,000
24

26. Phillip G. Akin
Duds N Suds Corp.
Laundry
Ames, IA
23
November 1980
19
3 Years at Iowa State University
$10,000,000
50–60

27. Julie Brice
Bill Brice Jr.
I Can't Believe Its Yogurt, Inc.
Food
Dallas, TX
27/28
January 1977
18/20
SMU Business Student
1980/SMU Business
$10,000,000
35 Full Time/85 Part Time

28. Robert Dean II
Executive Services, Ltd.
Limousine
Alexandria, VA
20
January 1982
18

High school graduate
$8,200,000
0 (all independent contractors)

29. Scott Walker
World Travel Brokers Inc.
Travel
Alsip, Illinois
24
November 1985
23
High school, some college
$8,000,000
75

30. Ted Leonsis
Redgate Communications Corporation
Integrated Communications Service/Publishing
Vero Beach, FL
30
January 1982
26
Graduate of Georgetown University
$8,000,000
45

31. Beth Daskal
Tri-State Custom Coach, Inc.
Limousine
Suffern, NY
23
1981
18

BA George Washington
University
$8,000,000
35

32. Ron Grey
Energy Enterprises
Construction
Stanton, CA
23
1981
18
BS Business Entrepre-
neurial program, Univer-
sity of Southern Califor-
nia
$7,200,000
25–27

33. Terry Dorman
Dorman Bogdonoff Co.
Electronics
Andover, MA
29
1977
25
Phillips Academy High
School Graduate
$7,000,000
150

34. Jeffery J. Roloff
Central Data Corp.
Manufacturer of Com-
puter Boards
Champaign, IL
28
Jan 1975

18
Associate Electrical En-
gineering, 1977
$6,700,000
72

35. Paul Mariates
Walter Martin
Andy Udleson
Flying Foods
Foods
New York, NY
27/29/26
1982
23/25/22
University of Massachu-
setts, Hotel School/Uni-
versity of Massachusetts,
Hotel School/University
of Massachusetts
$5,750,000
50

36. Brett M. Kingstone
Steven J. Prato
Kingstone Prato, Inc.
Investment Banking
Boulder, CO
26/27
June 1984
24/25
BA, Stanford Economics/
MBA, University of Cal-
ifornia Berkeley 1980, Fi-
nance
$5,500,000
11

37. Michael Hines
    Alfred F. Gerriets, II
    Mikal & Company, Inc.
    Investment Banking
    New York, NY
    27/27
    Junior Nassau Commu-
    nity College, Garden City,
    New York/University of
    Pennsylvania
    $5,500,000
    8

38. Matthew M. Brown
    Collegiate Group
    Market Insulation
    Provo, UT
    28
    December 1983
    25
    Brigham Young Univer-
    sity
    $5,210,000
    250

39. Michael Brown
    Central Point Software
    Computer Software
    Portland, OR
    28
    May 1981
    23
    High school, 3 years of
    college
    $5,180,447
    40

40. James R. Russo
    2nd Play Video

Video
West Los Angeles, CA
27
October 1983
25
Monica Jr. College, 1 yr.
Union County College/1
yr. Santa Monica Junior
College
$5,000,000
15

41. Michael Renna
    Michael Angelo's Gour-
    met Food Inc.
    Food
    Carlsbad, CA
    25
    1982
    20
    High school graduate
    $5,000,000
    30

42. Michael Macke
    Mike Pace
    Digital Controls, Inc.
    Video Games
    Norcross, GA
    30/28
    April 1981
    26/23
    Some college (Georgia
    State & Kennesaw Col-
    lege)/High school
    $5,000,000
    65

43. Yale Brozen
    Access International

Charter
New York, NY
22
1983
19
Columbia University
$5,000,000
10

44. Neil Balter
California Closet Company
Design/Construction
Woodland Hill, CA
25
January 1978
18
Some college; 2 years marketing major
$5,000,000
40 company owned; 500 franchise

45. Gary Peisach
Desserts Inc.
Food
Baltimore, MD
28
1978
21
University of Maryland, 1975–1977
$4,300,000
110

46. William Noble
William Noble Rare Jewels
Jewelry

Dallas, TX
30
January 1983
28
TCU BA: SMU MBA Program 1.5 semesters
$4,000,000
9

47. Scott Deperro
Aim Executive Inc.
Office Service
Cleveland, OH
29
1977
21
BBA, 1979, Kent State University, Ohio
$4,000,000
46

48. Steven Byer
Michael Cullina
Saladalley Restaurants
Food
Philadelphia, PA
30/30
January 1978
23/23
Tufts Graduate/Harvard Graduate
$4,000,000
250–300

49. Joel Billings
Strategic Simulations
Computer Software
Mountain View, CA
27

August 1979
22
Claremont, BS
$4,000,000
32

50. Jeff Frankel
I Love Yogurt Corp.
Food
Dallas, TX
23
June 1980
18
2.5 years UT, Austin;
1 year UT, Dallas
$3,750,000
125–150

51. Darius Azari
Chris Goode
Eric Goode
Shawn Hausman
Area Nightclub
New York, NY
26, 27, 28, 29
June 1982
22, 23, 24, 25
High school, B.A. New
York University, high
school—some college
$3,500,000
100 (full and part time)

52. Edmond Jette
University Computer
Stores, Inc.
Computer Retail Sales
Boston, MA
25

June 1984
23
BA, Northwestern University
$3,500,000
15

53. Edwin P. Berlin, Jr.
Cubicomp Corporation
Computer Graphics
Berkeley, CA
28
March 2, 1982
24
BS, EE Massachusetts Institute of Technology
$3,400,000
50

54. Barry Minkow
ZZZZ Best Carpet and
Furniture Co., Inc.
Home Furnishings
Reseda, CA
19
March 1981
16
High school, attending
night class
$3,300,000
125

55. Jacquelin LaColla
Barbara Leutert
Lela Computer Suitors
Computer Programming
& System Design
Clifton Park, NY
28/26

1982
22/21
MA. Engineering, BS, MBA, Rennsalaer Polytechnic/BS, Computer Science, Rennsalaer
$3,200,000
25

56. Jim Stein
Direct Language Publishing Inc.
Publishing Co.
San Francisco, CA
27
November 1982
25
High school dropout
$3,000,000
61

57. Karen Pohn
Interpro
Jewelry Importer & Exporter
Northfield, IL
27
November 1983
25
BS Finance, University of Colorado, Judicial Law
$3,000,000
7

58. Robert Kotick
Howard Marks
Arktronics
Developer Computer Software

Ann Arbor, MI
22/23
May 1983
20/19
Working on BA: General University Michigan/ University of Michigan Undergrads
$3,000,000
20–30

59. David Hedman
EPI-Center, Inc.
Earthquake Awareness
Palo Alto, CA
29
March 1981
25
AB Stanford; almost MS in Industrial Engineering
$3,000,000
40

60. Richard Garriott
Robert Garriott
Origin Systems, Inc.
Manufacturer Computer Software
Machests, NH
23/29
March 1983
21/26
High School: 2 years at University of Texas/BS, Electrical Engineering; BA Economics; MA, Electrical Engineering; MA Sloan
$3,000,000
25

61. Bob Day
    The Trade Arranger, Inc.
    Trading Exchange
    Indianapolis, IN
    26
    December 1980
    21
    BS Administration, Indiana University
    $3,000,000
    13

62. Michael Slewruk
    Hotlines Inc.
    Advertising
    Clearwater, FL
    28
    1983
    26
    BS Management
    $2,600,000
    11

63. Kevin Harrington
    Small Business Center/
    Franchise America
    Office Service
    Santa Monica, CA
    29
    January 1982
    25
    High school, 2 years college
    $2,500,000
    13

64. Brad Baker
    Tech: Time Inc.
    Computerized   Time
    Clocks
    Nokomis, FL
    26
    March 1984
    24
    University of Michigan
    one year; BS from Nova
    College
    $2,500,000
    15

65. Randall Pfeiffer
    Sandra Pfeiffer
    Genesis Electronics Corporation
    Electronics
    Folsom, CA
    29/29
    July 14, 1983
    26/26
    No degree/California
    State at Fullerton, BS
    Computer Science
    $2,000,000
    35

66. Juan Cameron, Jr.
    Home Maintenance Systems Inc.
    Contracting
    Washington, DC
    28
    February 1982
    24
    3.5 years at Boston University
    $2,200,000
    90

67. Frank Valente
    Cross-Valente Construc-
    tion Co.
    Construction
    Madira Beach, FL
    28
    January 1983
    25
    High school
    $2,000,000
    6

68. Peter Burns
    Burns Three Inc./Island
    Moped
    Moped & Bicycle Rental
    Sainbel Island, FL
    29
    1977
    19
    1986 Harvard Business
    School
    $2,000,000
    40

69. Donald Zabkar
    Zabs Backyard Hots
    Food
    Rochester, NY
    30
    January 1980
    25
    Grad Geneseo State
    $1,600,000
    120

70. Bill Epifanio, II
    Dynamedix Corp.
    Medical Technology

New York, NY
26
August 1982
23
AB Harvard
$1,500,000
15

71. Nick Colachis
    Jim Colachis
    Looking Good Publica-
    tions/VERTIGO
    Calendar Publishing/
    Nightclub
    Los Angeles, CA
    27, 27
    1981
    22, 22
    BA, University of South-
    ern California
    $1,340,000
    65 (full and part time)

72. Jordan G. Westropp
    Westropp Building Com-
    pany, Inc.
    Construction
    Cleveland, OH
    29
    1979
    23
    High school
    $1,300,000
    5

73. George M. Brostoff
    Symplex Communica-
    tions
    Data communications

equipment
Ann Arbor, MI
28
1981
23
University of Michigan,
Economics
$1,200,000
46

74. Heidi Wolf-Levinthal
Ketchum/New Venture
Communications
Advertising/Promotion
Palo Alto, CA
27
August 1982
25
BA Stanford
$1,200,000
21

75. Paul Klaassen
Sunrise Retirement
Homes
Real Estate
Oakton, VA
28
September 1981
24
Georgetown University
$1,200,000
55

76. Charles L. Frazier III
Digital Devices Corp.
Electronics
Atlanta, GA
26

June 1983
23
BBA-Accounting Georgia
State University
$1,010,000
0

77. Michael Reichwald
Brilliant Image
Computer Graphics
New York, NY
26
July 1983
24
BA, New York University;
Manager Economics &
Minor in Computer Sci-
ence; MBA-Baruch
$1,000,000
24

78. George W. Faison, Jr.
Ariane Daguin
D'Artagnon Inc.
Distributor & Manufac-
turer Food
Garfield, NJ
29/27
July 1984
27/26
BA, Spanish, Cum Laude-
Washington Lee Univer-
sity
$1,000,000
7

79. Raymond Haldeman
Raymond Haldeman Ca-
terers, Inc.

Food
Philadelphia, PA
28
January 1981
24
High school
$1,000,000
125

80. Tony Robbins
Robbins Research Institute
Personal Motivational Seminars, Fire Walking
Los Angeles, CA
26
1977
17
High school dropout
$1,000,000
4

81. Neal Elinoff
Neal's Cookies
Food
Houston, TX
30
October 1984
29
Medical School
$1,000,000
15

82. Steve Carb
Guiseppi's Inc.
Food
Hilton Head Island, NC
27
November 1981

22
BS Economics, Business Edinboro University, Edinboro, PA
$1,000,000
70 (most part time)

83. Todd Berstein
Corporate Telecom
Telephones
Van Nuys, CA
24
1980
18
2 Years at junior college/
Pierce
$1,000,000
12

84. Jerry Colclazier
J. W. Walker Company
Construction Management
Norman, OK
28
April 1984
27
Masters Health Care Administration, University of Oklahoma
$975,553
5

85. CeCe Colclazier
Equinox Entertainment Corp.
Entertainment
Norman, OK
29

April 1984
27
Bachelor of Arts, Interior
Design, University of
Oklahoma
$975,553
5

86. George J. Mandes
Health Care Technology
Corp.
Health Care
Hamden, CT
27
January 1982
23
Yale Public Health Grad-
uate School
$900,000
38

87. Jonathan Rotenberg
The Boston Computer
Society
Computer Consulting
Boston, MA
23
January 1977
15
Brown University; BA
Economics
$900,000
9

88. Rocky Enriquez
E & M Investments
Investments
Katy, TX

22
March 1985
21
High school
$900,000
5

89. Daniel P. Regenold
Posterservice, Inc.
Advertising
Kensington, MD
29
May 1983
26
B.S. Finance, Indiana
University, 1978, MBA
Xavier University, 1980
$750,000
12

90. Douglas J. Ranalli
Campus Publishing Inc.
Publishing
Upper Saddle River, NJ
24
November 1981
20
B.S. Engineering, Cornell
University 1983
$750,000
14

91. Mark David McKee
Pyramid Pizza
Food
Shawnee Mission, KS
24
1982

20
Kansas University Student
$750,000
90

92. David Looney
John Looney
Tar Heel Roofing
Construction
St. Petersburg, FL
23/28
1982
19/24
High school graduate
$700,000
15

93. Brian S. Peskin
Ultrawash
Truck washing
Houston, TX
29
1980
24
Massachusetts Institute of Technology
$600,000
30

94. Joseph Ford
Miss Ellie's Barbecue
Food
Chandler, AZ
26
November 1984
25
MBA, PHD Wichita State

University
$600,000
16

95. Sam Angus
Dan Bienenfeld
Design Look
Publishing
Agoura, CA
24/21
1981
21/18
Pre Law; University of California, at Santa Barbara/Student, University of Southern California
$505,000
4

96. Carol Phillips
Dermasystems
Beauty Care
Wichita, KS
25
October 1981
22
Wichita State
$500,000
11

97. Stuart Johnson
Network Consultants International (NCI)
Video on Health Foods
Newport Beach, CA
21
January 1986
21

High school
$500,000
5

98. John Herman
    The John Herman Co.,
    Inc.
    Specialty Advertising
    Cleveland, OH
    18
    January 1977
    10
    High school
    $500,000
    8

99. Phil Kosak
    KLB Enterprises
    Food

Greensboro, NC
29
August 1982
27
University of Georgia;
PHD Food Science
$500,000
1 + 3 Partners

100. Pat Somers
     Somer's Marketing
     Marketing
     Littleton, CO
     26
     October 1982
     22
     BA Business
     $485,000
     1

BIBLIOGRAPHY

BRANDT, STEVEN C. *Entrepreneuring*. Reading, Massachusetts: Addison Wesley Publishing Company, 1982.

CALANO, JAMES AND SALZMAN, JEFF. *Real World 101*. New York: Warner Books, 1982.

CAVANAUGH, RICHARD E. AND CLIFFORD, DONALD K., JR. *The Winning Performance*. New York: Bantam Books, 1985.

FISHOF, DAVID AND SHAPIRO, EUGENE. *Putting It On The Line*. New York: William Morrow & Co., 1983.

FRIEDMAN, MILTON AND ROSE. *Free To Choose*. New York: Harcourt Bruce Javanovich, 1979.

GILDER, GEORGE. *The Spirit of Enterprise*. New York: Simon and Schuster, 1984

GERVITZ, DON. *The New Entrepreneurs*. New York: Penguin Books, 1984.

KENT, CALVIN A., SEXTON, DONALD L. AND VESPER, KARL H. *Encyclopedia of Entrepreneurship*. Englewood Cliffs, New Jersey: Prentice Hall, 1982.

KINGSTONE, BRETT. *The Student Entrepreneur's Guide*. Berkeley: Ten Speed Press, 1981.

LEFEVRE, EDWIN. *Reminiscences of a Stock Operator*. Burlington, Vermont: Books of Wall Street, 1923.

LIPPER, ARTHUR III. *Venture's Guide to Investing in Private Companies*. Homewood, Illinois: Dow Jones Irwin, 1984.

MACHLOWITZ, MARILYN. *Whiz Kids*. New York: Arbor House, 1985.

PETERS, THOMAS J. AND WATERMAN, ROBERT H. *In Search of Excellence*. New York: Harper & Row, 1982.

REICH, CARY. *Financier: The Life Story of Andre Meyer*. William Morrow and Company, Inc. 1983.

251

SILVER, A. DAVID. *Entrepreneurial Megabucks*. New York: John Wiley and Sons, Inc., 1985.

THOMPSON, JAQUELINE. *Future Rich*. New York: William Morrow and Co., 1985.

VESPER, KARL M. *New Venture Strategies*. Englewood Cliffs, New Jersey: Prentice Hall, 1980.

INDEX

253